LEE J BRYAN

HOW SAFE IS YOUR VAPE?

T0386728

Future-proofing your brand through robust compliance

R^ethink

First published in Great Britain in 2023
by Rethink Press (www.rethinkpress.com)

© Copyright Lee Bryan

This book is dedicated to my son Freddie, who is the driver for everything I do, and to my mum Linda, to whom I owe everything, for believing in me and giving me my first start in business. Love you, Mum!

Contents

Foreword

Do you want your products to be on the market five years from now? That is the question I have heard Lee Bryan ask many businesses throughout the last few years, and it succinctly sums up how he and Arcus Compliance work. Lee and his company truly believe in the harm reduction potential of vape products and have spent many years developing processes and best practices to help smaller brands stand shoulder to shoulder with big tobacco companies, to ensure their products stay on the market and to build sustainable businesses. In short, if you want to stay in business, become and remain profitable, and safeguard your consumers, listen up.

Since vapour products were regulated in Europe back in 2016, Lee and his team have tirelessly acquired an ever-evolving body of knowledge, successfully monitored the increasing needs and requirements of the numerous competent authorities, and built continuously improved processes using their unique 'hive mind' approach. When one client experiences a particular issue, Arcus' team of specialists rapidly reviews that issue and rolls out the fix for their entire client portfolio. Such a simple principle has proven to increase the robustness of processes for much of the industry and has cemented Arcus' position as the leading authority on regulatory compliance.

I have personally known Lee since the early days of the vape industry's growth in the UK and came to work closely with him when he joined the UKVIA's standards committee several years ago. It was clear that his incisive insight into issues that his own clients were facing would also benefit the wider industry and this was proven with his involvement in developing the UKVIA's standards charter, designed to ensure consumer safety and boost confidence in vape products.

Lee's direct, no-nonsense approach has been a welcome breath of fresh air in an industry that emerged from the maverick beginnings of home-brewed, experimental products, through the wake of the Tobacco Products Directive, to what is now a multinational, professional sector empowering millions of smokers to make the switch to less harmful alternatives. This approach, along with Lee's vast expertise amassed from nearly a decade in the industry, is now encapsulated in this book and available to you, the aspiring entrepreneur.

As the industry attracts greater scrutiny from legislators and regulatory authorities across the globe, an effective and manageable compliance strategy has also become increasingly important. I have long campaigned and lobbied for pragmatic and sensible regulation that benefits, rather than restricts, trade and consumer choice, but the industry itself needs the tools to be able to play its part. The vaping industry's reputation – and future – depend on it.

I believe this book will be such a huge help to the ambitious challenger vapour brands around the world. By providing an effective roadmap on key aspects of their regulatory obligations, it will go a long way to keeping valuable diversity across the industry. Armed with this valuable blueprint, your business will undoubtedly be on the right track to success.

John Dunne, Managing Director, Dyflin Group Consulting, Director General, UK Vaping Industry Association (www.UKVIA.co.uk)

Introduction

Compliance may not be sexy, but neither is going to jail.

Long gone are the days when a 'compliance strategy' meant copying the labels of the industry's market leaders and hoping for the best. Europe and the UK are now several years into being a regulated market, with more industry regulations planned around the world. In 2016, when the Tobacco Products Directive came into force, the member state enforcement bodies were initially overwhelmed by the volume of notifications, but they have now caught up, are educated and are enforcing the rules. The health ministries are reviewing toxicological data and product formulations, customs forces are checking Safety Data Sheets and we've even heard of international courier companies refusing to ship nicotine-containing liquids.

A few months before writing this book, I had a call out of the blue from a big brand with a huge problem. They were a global brand who were earning 80% of their revenue from one of their flavours. (Sound familiar?) They had just received a letter from the local competent authority wishing to investigate their recipe data as the disclosed data looked a little 'light' on quantity. Upon investigation, it was found that one of the concentrates within the recipe contained banned substances and the product had to be removed from the market. The reformulation process took them six months, which saw them lose more than £600,000 in revenue.

How would a similar scenario affect you? Are you prepared for that inevitable knock at the door? Because I can tell you that it is inevitable. Every major vapour brand in the world that intends to place their products on the UK/NI market has to submit product notifications to the Medicines & Healthcare Products Regulatory Agency (MHRA), which has assembled a focus team to address the issue of regulatory compliance. As a submitter, you must legally stand by the accuracy of the information you have provided.

Yes, the screw is tightening, and if you want to survive as a vape manufacturer in the current regulatory landscape, you need to have a robust compliance strategy that includes ongoing monitoring and improvements. Just because you are compliant today, doesn't mean you will be in six months from now. How quickly can you adapt to changes in regulations? It's a moving target and you have to keep readjusting to maintain that compliant status. Make no mistake, regulatory compliance can bury your business. In today's regulatory environment, compliance needs to be taken as seriously as marketing.

It can be done, however, and it doesn't need to be expensive, either. With a little time and effort, and in some cases some professional advice, you will be able to build your due diligence and futureproof your brand and company. Most importantly, you will keep your products on the shelves and selling.

How Safe is Your Vape? will show you what you need to know, what you need to do and how best to do it. It will show you what you can do easily inhouse and what you can't. And, if you can't, how to find the right people to do it for you. *How Safe is Your Vape?* will provide you with a roadmap that will keep you on the path of compliance, consumer safety and continued profitability.

I joined the vape industry in 2013 after spending much of my early career in the leather chemical industry, working on white label projects for some of the most prestigious car, sofa, shoe and handbag brands in the world. I wanted a change of career and had been monitoring the electronic cigarette industry for a while. It appealed to me greatly from a technological standpoint, but more so from a harm reduction perspective.

Having lost my father, grandfather and grandmother to smoking-related illnesses, I realised that their deaths could have been prevented if vaping had been around twenty or thirty years ago. I didn't come into the vape industry being passionate about it, but my passion for it grew from that. I saw anything that could loosen big tobacco's grasp on consumers as a big positive and wanted to make sure that the industry at large was doing everything it possibly could to raise the bar. I saw the potential that vaping had in terms of its ability to create a smoke-free generation.

I started with the largest e-liquid manufacturer in the world, joining them to re-launch and develop a failing mass market brand, and turned it around within six short months. On the back of that success, I won a multi-million-pound contract with a Scandinavian brand looking to break into the vaping sector.

Spending time with the compliance team of the Scandinavian client made me realise that regulatory compliance was going to have a massive impact on the vape industry. Unfortunately (or fortunately, as it turned out), my boss didn't share my vision. In 2017, my team and I started our own company, Arcus Compliance, with the aim of blending the experience we'd gained in the vape industry with our proven software development skills to create a set of tools that would allow even small brands to compete on a level playing field (at least from a compliance perspective). It was a methodology that was simple enough for a 'mom and pop' operation to implement, yet robust enough to stand up as part of a due diligence process with the appropriate member state authorities.

Arcus has more than twenty-five years' experience in the vaping industry, spread across manufacturing, retail and regulatory compliance, and we sit on the standards committee of the UK Vaping Industry Association. We have successfully built and implemented global compliance strategies for many of the largest brands in the industry. We offer a complete range of regulatory and compliance solutions and we have developed a range of vape-focused software tools that have dramatically reduced compliance costs in the industry.

Principal among these is our unique CORE compliance system, which will be explained in this book. Using it, you will be able to ring-fence your products with proven processes and demonstrate due diligence to any enquiring member state, authority or interested client.

I'll show you point by point the aspects you need to consider to ensure that you not only create robust compliance files to demonstrate your due diligence and manage your product stewardship, but you also add value to your brand by improving your reputation and intellectual property in readiness for any interested investors or buyers.

After reading this book you will have the knowledge to sell your products even in the most highly regulated and highly enforced markets, knowing that they will comply with all the relevant regulations.

Important note

This book is written in layman's terms to help non-technical, non-scientific brand owners better understand their baseline obligations. It is not a bible, it is not a replacement for reading and understanding the regulations, it is not an exhaustive and foolproof method, nor is it a substitute for hiring specialist consultancies or legal representation, which remain essential if you are to safeguard your business and build your brand. It will, however, provide you with a basic and clear roadmap of what you need to do to become and remain fully compliant, protecting your products and your company for the long term.

PART ONE
COMPLIANCE AND THE LAW

If you want to survive as a vape manufacturer in the current regulatory landscape, you need to have a robust compliance strategy that includes ongoing monitoring and improvements. Just because you are compliant today, you won't necessarily still be in six months' time. Compliance is a moving target and you have to keep readjusting your aim to maintain your compliant status. This is where many brands fall down: they do the bare minimum, rather than constantly reviewing the compliance landscape to ensure that their products remain safe and fit for purpose.

In Part 1, we'll look at the rules and regulations that you need to be aware of, the advantages of compliance (and the penalties you can incur if you don't get it right), and a simple four-step process that will help you ensure you stay on the right side of the law, both now and in the future.

ONE
What Are The Rules?

The pioneers of the vape industry were very much entrepreneurs. They thought quickly and developed products that would sell without necessarily considering everything that might be required for a regulated market. There wasn't one. A decade on, many people in the industry still assume that the only thing they need to worry about is the Tobacco Products Directive (TPD).[1] But today, the regulatory landscape is a maze of multiple regulations, making it difficult to navigate.

In fact, depending on your product type – whether it is an e-liquid or a device – there are as many as fifteen regulations that will impact your business. You will

1   https://health.ec.europa.eu/system/files/2016-11/dir_201440_en_0.pdf

need to consider how you engineer your products, how they are classified, labelled and packaged, how they are marketed and what market surveillance you have in place. The more countries you buy from and sell into, the more red tape you will become entangled in. For example, while the UK doesn't (currently) stipulate an international standard for emissions, the UAE does.

The regulations that apply to your business will also depend on its size, ie, whether it is a corporation or a small- or medium-sized enterprise (SME). Being an SME is a godsend when it comes to the way most EU member states treat you.

There still seems to be a belief among some brands that there is strength in numbers and they can hide in the masses. While case law may stand a chance of helping the industry in the US, and the Far East is still largely unregulated, it is not going to be that way for much longer (in 2022, China implemented a licensing requirement for vape companies) and it certainly isn't the case in Europe.

Though the majority of brands in the industry have realised this, many are still not doing enough to meet their compliance obligations. A lot of it is quite simple, such as making sure that you are considering the requirements for a particular market – whether that be Europe, the Middle East or the States – and that, when you are developing new products, you have made a list of considerations that need to be taken into account first.

In this chapter, we'll look at some of the rules and regulations you need to be aware of for different markets, how they have evolved and continue to evolve. (We'll look at possible future developments in regulation in the next chapter.)

Unregulated beginnings

The first electronic cigarette was patented as far back as 1927, though it was never commercialised. It wasn't until 2003 that what would become the first commercially successful electronic nicotine delivery system (ENDS) – otherwise known as vapour or vape product – was created, in China. It was called Ruyan (meaning 'like smoke') and it caught on. Within three years, the idea had spread to Europe and the US and vaping became a worldwide phenomenon.

In the UK, conventional tobacco smoking had just been banned in workplaces and public buildings, and e-cigarettes seemed like the next big thing – especially in parts of the country with a tradition of heavy industry and heavy smoking. The initial boom took place in the Northwest of England, South Wales and other areas with a history of shipbuilding and mining. The pioneers knew their market and were going to capitalise on it.

They were mainly market traders and tradespeople, with no technical, scientific or professional background and little concern with ensuring that their products met any legal standards or restrictions that might apply to them. In any case, the only regulations that then applied to the sale of tobacco products related to advertising restrictions and packaging requirements. Flavour concentrates were coming from China with little or no testing and there was absolutely no testing on the final products. A lot of those pioneers even used food additives or flavourings in vape products, while others simply looked at what the number one brand in the industry was doing and copied that. It wasn't quite the Wild West, but close to it.

Once the regulations did hit, those who had recruited wisely and hired scientific, technical and quality-control managers were able to continue growing, while those that hadn't stagnated or even exited the market.

When I entered the vape industry in 2013, there was still little or nothing in the way of regulation that applied directly to it, but I could already see what was on the horizon. It was clear to me that regulatory compliance was about to have a massive impact on the vape industry, so I began looking for people to help the company I worked for build a compliance strategy. Having found what appeared to be the most well-prepared and well-funded contract manufacturer and compliance company in Europe, I became its global sales manager and the rest of my team quickly joined me.

Within a week, however, it was clear that we had joined a very 'well presented' company, but one that had no clients and no clue. Worse, it had links to Big Tobacco, which meant that nobody wanted to talk to us, let alone give us business. My once hugely successful team couldn't even get a meeting. Needless to say, this didn't last long and they dispensed with our services after only a few months.

Coincidentally, this was the year of the TPD, which changed both the vape industry and my life.

The Tobacco Products Directive (TPD)

The TPD, enforced by the EU Commission in 2014 and effective in all EU Member States (including the UK) from May 2016, placed restrictions on the content, strength and quantity of liquids in e-cigarettes, as well as imposing requirements regarding their design, packaging and labelling. In the UK, the sale of all e-cigarettes and e-liquids had to be notified to the MHRA.

At this time, I was consulting for a compliance company that, again, seemed to know what it was doing. In reality, it was only damaging its own reputation – and mine – so I left. I was planning to buy a chain of vape stores when one of the company's clients called me and said, 'I heard you're going. Maybe it's time you set up your own shop?' I had a private equity investor ready to back me and my business partner to buy ten shops in Wales. I didn't want to let the opportunity go and take the risk of making it on my own as a consultant, so I asked, 'Are you saying that if I set my own shop up, you'll come with me?' He said, 'Yeah.' I now had an offer of a £150,000-a-year contract in a business that wouldn't require me that much.

I considered the pros and cons of the two offers and then, two days before I was due to sign the deal with the private equity firm, they pulled out. The decision had been made for me: I was going to be working in compliance. It was never my dream. It was never something that I'd even wanted to do. But this client obviously wanted to retain our services. They wanted us to hold their hand and take away all the aggravation of compliance. So, Arcus Compliance was born.

I soon discovered that a subscription or retainer model was what companies wanted. Initially, our focus was to provide accurate and complete TPD notifications for the industry. When the TPD came into force, a lot of savvy manufacturers quickly saw a loophole in the Directive that allowed them to remove the nicotine content from their e-liquids and continue to sell it, thereby steering clear of costly notifications. But there is a lot more to the regulations than a limit on nicotine content. For example, the TPD requires companies to record all adverse events related to their products, which many were simply unable to do. Besides, while removing nicotine means you are not obliged to notify your e-liquids in the majority of European member states (although some still require you to), there are other 'catch-all' regulations that require you to maintain a certain level of safety, the main one being the General Product Safety Directive and member state transpositions of this.

The spread of regulation

Europe was the first region in the world to regulate vape products, in 2016. For the first couple of years, there was a paper-shuffling exercise. The European Parliament had landed twenty-eight countries with a set of new regulations to implement, but each country first wanted to see who the players were in the market, what products they had, what consumers wanted, what flavours were the most popular – and what chemicals within those flavours could be harmful to consumers.

During this period, there were unscrupulous manufacturers who would simply sign a Declaration of Conformity (with the TPD) without having done any due diligence, knowing that it would only become a problem if a member state – or competent authority within that state – actually checked it. They also knew that a lot of member states didn't have the resources to check everything (some still don't) and the EU's Common Entry Gateway system (EU-CEG) itself didn't have the functionality to be able to validate the data. It was hit and miss as to what was actually checked.

I spent the first two years after Arcus was formed working on short-term contracts with some of the largest retailers and vapour brands in the world. Those two years were crammed full of insightful experiences. What most impressed me was the 'little' guys who were trying to do it right; who had started with a single vape shop and, like me, a commitment to quit tobacco; who were travelling the world with boxes of e-liquid and bags of passion – guys who are still shaping our industry.

They were the ones that needed the regulatory help and economical solutions to ever-increasing compliance headaches. I was tired of the smoke and mirrors that I had experienced from the major players. I was tired of the big companies pretending that compliance was a dark art and trying to charge exorbitant prices for simple solutions. I wanted my company to deliver compliance services, training and tools that allowed clients to pick and choose how much help they needed.

Essentially, what they wanted was peace of mind. But I realised back then that they weren't ready to implement standards themselves (and, in doing so, raise the bar of the vape industry), which was frustrating, because I could see the need for this. Vape had to poke a stick at Big Tobacco because those guys had the money to outlast anyone. If we didn't up our game, our industry would crash and burn.

Thankfully the vape industry did, and still is thriving today – and it looks like it is going to continue for a long time. There are still hurdles to jump and we will be looking into those and how to get over them.

As the market has matured and the 'education' of the competent authorities has developed, their desire for improved consumer preference data has increased and there is now a flow of sales data that allows both the authorities and the manufacturers to build a picture of customer preferences in terms of flavours and device designs, although a compendium of data on average numbers of puffs taken and quantities of liquid consumed are probably still a few years away.

Other industries

As we progressed, we realised that baseline compliance tended to be similar not only for each new regulation but also for each new industry.

A lot of the vape guys had transitioned into hemp or recreational and medicinal cannabis. And once we started looking into the regulations that applied to products such as cannabidiol (CBD), we saw similarities in quality management, risk management, product data, and so on. The same compliance principles could be applied here, as well as to the sex toys industry.

But the focus of this book is on the vape industry, so let's look in more detail at the main regulations that apply to it.

The EU

For products sold within the European Union, notifications must be made through the European Common Entry Gateway system. As part of that notification, manufacturers must submit a Declaration of Conformity, which essentially confirms that they have done their due diligence and everything within that notification is safe for consumers and the intended use of the product.

Generally speaking, however, EU (and many UK) regulations do not stipulate exactly what needs to be done in order to conform to them; that is left largely to the manufacturer or producer to determine. This puts the onus very much on them to be aware of all the marks, directives, standards and so on that apply (or might apply) to their products. Here is a summary of some of these:

CE mark C€

The familiar CE mark stands for 'conformité euro-péenne' – European conformity – and is applied to various types of products, from toys and machinery to explosive devices. These include vape products.

There are around seventeen European directives that require specific products to carry the CE mark. The two that principally apply to vape products are Electromagnetic Compatibility (EMC) Directive 2014/30/EU and The Restriction of Hazardous Substances (RoHS) Directive 2002/95/EC, which are discussed briefly below.

There are also regulations regarding how the CE mark appears on the product or its packaging. For example, the minimum height of the mark is 5mm, which means that, if a device is small, it may be displayed on the leaflet, user manual or packaging.

RoHS

The RoHS Directive, which has been in effect since 2006, restricts the use of ten hazardous materials – including lead, chromium and certain plasticisers – in the manufacture of various types of electronic and electrical equipment, including vape products.

EMC

The latest EMC Directive, which came into force in 2014, limits electromagnetic emissions from equipment in order to ensure that it does not disturb radio and telecommunication signals and is itself immune to interference.

RED

Vape devices can also be subject to the Radio Equipment Directive (RED) 2014/53/EU (effective from 2017) if, for example, they are linked to a mobile phone app that monitors things like your puff duration and the airflow through the device.

EN

Any vape device sold in the EU must comply with the relevant European Standard (confusingly abbreviated to EN, from the German for European standard, Europäische Norm).

CLP

The Classification, Labelling and Packaging Regulation introduced in 2008 aligned the EU system to the Globally Harmonised System in order to facilitate global trade. According to the CLP Regulation, your products are classified in terms of their level of hazard, which in turn determines the hazard statements, signal words and pictograms that must be displayed on the labelling or packaging to communicate the potential hazard to the consumer. We'll be looking at these in Chapter 8.

REACH

Another relevant EU regulation is the Registration, Evaluation, Authorisation and Restriction of Chemicals (REACH). This is applied by the European Chemicals Agency (ECHA), which is responsible for ensuring that companies are using chemicals safely, providing the necessary information on them and addressing concerns related to their use. The ECHA also assists companies in determining their CLP classification (see above).

Marketing and surveillance

Yet another EU regulation (no. 765/2008) sets out the requirements for market surveillance of vape (and other) products. These affect not only your after-sales surveillance (see Chapter 9), but also your distribution system, your imports and your contracts with suppliers.

Technical file

For a product to be given a CE mark, the application must be accompanied by a technical file containing information on the product design (and the logic behind it), the packaging, any instruction manuals and so on. (In fact, there is no set list of what the technical file should contain.)

The technical file should be available to any member state surveillance authority and should be retained on file for at least ten years from the point of the first product going on the market.

Country variations

The TPD is the minimum standard that all EU member states must impose, but each state is at liberty to 'gold plate' it with additional stipulations when they transpose it into local law. Germany, for example, has added substances to its banned chemicals list, while Denmark insists that all devices must be childproofed.

This means that it isn't enough to be conversant with the TPD; you must also be au fait with the specific regulations and requirements in each country into which you are selling your products.

The UK

Until 31 January 2020, the UK was subject to EU regulations. Post-Brexit, the MHRA had to build its own notification system, which, though far from perfect, is a lot better than the EU Common Entry Gate system. It does have built-in validation, which means that you won't get a validation unless the appropriate data are submitted, including chemical profiles and toxicological search results. Once your notification is valid and you have paid the notification fee, your notification will be reviewed to ensure the data is adequate. Your product will then be included on the next published list.

In general, the MHRA is more supportive of the vape industry than any of the other European markets or European competent authorities. This may be for purely economic reasons. After all, we are paying for a public health service and the science indicates that vaping is safer than combustible tobacco, so it makes sense for the UK population to be vaping rather than smoking.

And the UK 'polices' itself better than almost any other country in the world. It has strong industry associations, such as the UK Vaping Industry Association (UKVIA), which ensure that their members comply with all the relevant regulations and, even if a brand is not a member, will 'refer' it to the competent authority if they think that it may not be compliant.

More importantly, the associations have a positive attitude towards harm reduction, moving consumers away from combustibles rather than purely being interested in the industry earning money.

Some of the UK regulations that need to be adhered to are described briefly below:

TRPR

The Tobacco and Related Products Regulations (TRPR) transposed the relevant stipulations of the TPD for the UK market. The TRPR includes sections that are specific to vaping products.

UKCA **UK CA**

As regards the marking of products, when the UK left the EU, it was no longer allowed to use the CE mark, so it had to develop its own, which is called the UKCA (UK Conformity Assessed) mark.

To obtain a UKCA mark, a product must be tested by a 'notified' or approved body such as Intertek or the BSI.

While some UK products must be put through a Conformity Assessment process in order to carry the mark on the product, packaging and documentation, vape products are currently self-assessed and self-certified, which means that it is up to you to ensure that the product is properly tested and complies with all relevant standards and regulations.

Obviously, if you were totally unscrupulous, you could just apply a UKCA (or even CE) mark without doing any compliance or testing at all and nobody would know (unless there was a problem), but, as I will explain in the rest of this book, this is simply not an option if you want to take your business and the safety of the consumer seriously.

Strangely, the CE mark still applies in Northern Ireland, which operates under something called the Northern Ireland Protocol, so that products often carry two different marks, although there is no regulatory requirement for this.

Other markets

Space precludes a description of all the regulations that apply in other world markets, which range from almost completely unregulated (eg, South Africa) to stringently controlled (eg, the United Arab Emirates).

In the US, for example, where there is (still) no public health system and Big Tobacco (still) has enormous influence, the regulatory situation is almost the polar opposite of what we see in the UK. For example, it has only a voluntary mark, the FCC (Federal Communications Commission), which indicates that the electromagnetic radiation from the device is below the limits specified by the FCC.

The UAE, on the other hand, have taken the TPD as the basis of their regulatory system and 'gold plated' it. For example, whereas the TPD requires you to have written procedures in terms of quality management, it doesn't stipulate that these must meet an international standard. The same goes for emissions testing and the testing of e-liquids. To pass muster in the UAE, however, your quality management system needs to be ISO 9001 and your lab needs to be accredited to ISO 17025 for emissions testing. By the way, in future iterations of the TPD we might see international standards being applied, so this could be something to anticipate.

Summary

- The days of simply copying what other brands were doing or sticking conformity marks on vape products and hoping for the best are long gone.

- European and many other countries have devised multiple regulations to control the production and sale of vape products and are now enforcing them rigorously.

- As a manufacturer, you need to be aware of the regulations that apply to your products and develop a robust compliance strategy to ensure that you not only are compliant today, but also maintain your compliant status into the future.

- Compliance need not be merely a 'necessary evil'.

- The need for compliance applies equally to other products.

TWO

Why Comply?

The simple answer is that you *must* comply, because it is the law of the land (or the law of the industry if you prefer) and there are often severe penalties for non-compliance.

However, there is another, even more important reason. As more and more countries began to implement regulations for the vapour industry, it became clear that they all had a common theme: consumer protection. The rules and directives that have been put in place are not only to ensure that your products are fit for purpose, but also – in fact, primarily – to ensure the relative safety of the consumer.

The key consideration is whether you perceive that requirement to be a burden or an opportunity, because there are advantages to be gained from compliance, as well as penalties that can be incurred through non-compliance.

Consumer safety

Just as it is consumers who have largely driven the trends in vaping – initially towards simple, cigarette-like devices, then to refillable tanks and bigger devices, mods that generated clouds of vape and, more recently, full circle back to smaller, disposable devices – the need for compliance has essentially been driven by consumer safety.

Conformité européenne, for example (see Chapter 1), requires manufacturers to build a technical file of all of the testing, risk assessments and other procedures they have carried out to ensure that their products have been adequately tested and are safe for the consumer to use. There are also marketing and sur-veillance regulations and directives which stipulate what you must do to monitor that use after you have sold the product in order to ensure that any consumer safety issues are swiftly identified and acted upon (see Chapter 9).

In other words, there must be full traceability so that you can provide the enforcement bodies with information on who is legally responsible for the safety of your products in each region and country where they are sold. In our business, for example, we have seen products with a high liquid or tank capacity or a high nicotine content that were initially destined for the US making their way into Europe, where they will contravene regulations. Without adequate traceability, your products can be forcibly recalled and you not only lose sales, but also suffer reputational damage.

Brand reputation and competitive advantage

Acquiring and maintaining a reputation, in any field, means building trust – among your suppliers, your customers and, not least, the authorities. This last aspect is often overlooked, but it is crucial to achieving competitive advantage in the marketplace.

There is increasing demand from consumers to know what is in their liquids and how safe they are. Increasingly, consumers know what a safe device or product needs to contain or look like and what needs to be on the packaging, etc. Even if you think you can 'get round' the authorities, you will have difficulty deceiving the people who are ultimately buying your products.

In the UK recently, there were reports in the media of certain brands causing nosebleeds and other health impacts. In such cases, retailers and wholesalers might decide to steer clear of those brands, with potentially disastrous effects not only on short-term sales, but also on long-term reputation.

However, there are also reputational *advantages* to meeting the authorities' demands. By making sure that you build solid compliance files, that all the data in those files are available to downstream users, that your information is in all the necessary languages and that you are aware of all the nuances in regulation across the different EU member states, for example – particularly if you are a market leader – you are much more likely to turn the enforcement bodies or competent authorities on their heels. Once they have made an initial investigation, they will be satisfied that you know what you have to do and are doing it correctly. Remember: these guys are human too, and if they see that you have your ship in order, they are more likely to leave you in peace.

Compliance can be an opportunity – a marketing tool that you can use to your advantage. It is in your interest to not only ensure that your compliance is comprehensive and up to date, but also to 'sing' about the fact that you are complying with the relevant electrical and tobacco- or nicotine-specific regulations. Informing your consumers and all downstream users (including distributors, wholesalers and retailers) will help you to build their trust.

Enforcement

We are now seven years along the road of being a regulated industry and the authorities have caught up and are enforcing on brands who break the rules. They are working on a steady stream of intelligence from within the industry and are taking a focused approach – a sniper rifle rather than a shotgun.

There are different layers of enforcement. In the UK, for example, while the MHRA scrutinises the notifications that have been made for tobacco products, either removing them entirely or asking for further information to ensure that the products pass muster (under its Yellow Card system), Trading Standards and the Office of Product Standards and Safety (OPSS) have enforcement teams that visit retailers and can seize any non-compliant products.

Because there are now thousands of brands on the UK market, the competent authorities rely on businesses completing a Declaration of Conformity. In signing this, the brand owner or manufacturer confirms that they understand their obligations, that they are aware of the regulations, that their products meet the required level of safety and that they themselves are achieving an acceptable level of compliance. The enforcement bodies then carry out spot checks, and if they find something that isn't right, they will conduct an investigation. If this reveals other issues, they may take the matter to the MHRA, or even the courts, or simply remove the product from the market.

If a problem with the product becomes apparent as a result of consumer feedback or complaints, the MHRA might issue a Yellow Card. If they then proceed to conduct an investigation and find that the business hasn't conducted due diligence or is knowingly marketing an unsafe product, they might institute criminal proceedings.

Elsewhere in Europe, the enforcement bodies are generally a lot stricter than in the UK. In Germany, for example, they will go round trade exhibitions seizing products and issuing warning notices or fines to companies exhibiting products that don't comply with their country-specific regulations.

Even if it might be the distributor or retailer that ultimately incurs the penalties, you will suffer reputational damage as the brand owner.

Penalties

The penalties for non-compliance can be severe. In the UK, for example, companies that break the rules can be fined up to £20,000 per instance. Where non-compliance is shown to cause harm, individuals can receive up to two-year custodial sentences – though thankfully that has not happened yet.

There is another kind of 'penalty' that can be equally damaging – and it is far more common. We have personally had at least half a dozen such cases in the last five years.

Very often, a brand will make 80% of its revenue – maybe as much as £600,000 a year – from just two of its flavours. In some cases, when it comes to submitting a compliance file for the relevant products, we discover that one of these flavours is non-compliant. Overnight, the company is no longer able to sell those products. They must reformulate them to meet the regulations, which can take three months or more. This means they are facing a loss of at least £150,000 in revenue. We have even had companies losing more than a million pounds simply because they hadn't checked that a particular concentrate or flavour was fully compliant.

It is no longer enough simply to develop a flavour that smells good and vapes well; you must now consider what it contains at the molecular level and whether those ingredients are on the 'green' or 'white' list of chemicals that are permitted in a particular region or country. In 2017, for example, just after the enforcement of the TPD, a lot of popular flavours – custards and creams – were found to contain the banned substances diacetyl and acetaldehyde. This led to a rapid change in many brands' range of flavours – in this case, a change driven by regulation rather than by consumer demand. But it took the flavour houses quite a while to develop new flavours (and to replicate the old custard cream flavours without using diacetyl and acetaldehyde). A lack of foresight and awareness of impending compliance issues therefore caused a lot of unnecessary revenue loss.

A similar issue can arise in complex flavours. Many popular flavours are now quite complex. A 'summer fruits' flavour, for example, won't simply be a mix of one strawberry and one blackberry flavour. It might have three or four different strawberries and two or three different blackberries, to give it that 'wow factor' that makes the difference between a product that sells in the thousands and one that sells in the millions. However, because there could be only a very small quantity of 'blackberry 3' in each mix, the flavour house might suddenly decide that its manufacture is no longer viable, so they cease production – and bang goes your 'wow factor'.

A related issue is that flavour houses often won't release the exact chemical make-up of their individual flavours (their Chemical Abstracts Service or CAS numbers) to their clients or won't go to the expense of carrying out a full toxicological assessment of each chemical ingredient, but will simply issue a toxicological 'monograph' (which is essentially a library search of all of the studies that have been made on that chemical). This can mean that, when you combine several flavours, although individually they may be below the threshold for declaration to the authorities, the combination of them exceeds that threshold and exposes you to potential penalties.

You might think there is nothing you can do about all this, but there is. We'll be seeing how in Part 2 of this book.

The future of regulation

There is little doubt that regulation of the vape industry will become tighter in the future – and quite likely the near future. Generally speaking, we expect that brands will be required to submit more robust assessments of their products.

For example, I have just mentioned the issue of toxicological assessments vs toxicological monographs – the latter only currently being required by the MHRA in the UK. As the industry and the competent authorities mature, we shall probably see a requirement for qualified toxicologist reports for each product. That will be expensive, but with the likely shrinking of the number of companies in the industry, there will be a bigger slice of the pie for each of them in terms of revenue. Successful brands will probably need to invest in that area, which is something to start considering now.

Other changes of focus that we are already seeing concern labelling and packaging, and the classification of the hazard of the product. As we have said, gone are the days of simply 'copying' what the leading brands are doing. Companies are increasingly engaging professional support in this area and using the ECHA tables to determine the appropriate CLP classification, which, as we shall see in Chapter 8, can be a complex task in the case of liquids with multiple flavours.

On the subject of flavours, some EU member states have recently banned all vape flavours except tobacco and menthol, and it is possible that other countries will follow suit.

Poland recently became the first EU member state to make it mandatory to undertake consumer studies for vape products (see Consumer studies in Chapter 9), and it is likely that the requirement for consumer studies to be carried out will scale up as the regulations mature.

Last, but not least, in future iterations of the TPD we may see international standards being applied. This is already the case in the United Arab Emirates, where e-liquid testing has to be conducted by an ISO 17025-accredited laboratory. Your testing may, for example, have to be carried out using a stability chamber. If you happen to have one of these in your manufacturing facility, great, but because of the time period required for an adequate test and the fact that the stability chamber has to be monitored twenty-four hours a day (even then, they can be unpredictable), you will usually need to outsource your testing to a third party, which can be costly.

To save money, some companies do a short-term stability test such as a three-month accelerated test, from which they try to predict the product's shelf life – or even simply use the standard shelf life given to them by the nicotine manufacturers – but, again, regulations in this area are likely to be tightened up, so this is another thing to consider going forwards.

In fact, in 2021, the MHRA held a consultative meeting to consider tightening the regulations concerning emissions and testing. For example, if one of your products is labelled as having a shelf life of twelve months, you may in future be asked to justify how you arrived at that figure.

Another impending change to EU regulations is that the 'Unique Formula Identifier' (UFI – see Chapter 8) will become mandatory on the label of all products classified as containing health or physical hazards from 2025.

There is little doubt that compliance will play an increasing part in whether brands succeed or fail. If you are not complying with the regulations, your product won't be on the shelves for long. And while over-regulation is never a good thing, a well-balanced regulatory landscape will self-police and have the effect of ridding the industry of brands that flout the rules, leaving bigger slices of the pie to the guys who are doing it right.

Summary

- Compliance is no longer an option, so it is up to you to be aware of the regulations, requirements and standards that apply to your products.

- The penalties for non-compliance in terms of fines, and even prison sentences, can be severe.

- Consumer safety is an even more important reason for compliance than avoiding penalties.

- Non-compliance can also result in considerable reputational damage.

- On the other hand, compliance can give your company a competitive advantage.

- If you are seen to be making efforts to be compliant, the authorities will likely 'leave you be' and you will develop the trust of your clients and customers.

- There is little doubt that regulation will become tighter in future, so it is in your interest to establish a robust compliance strategy now.

THREE
What Is CORE Compliance?

CORE Compliance™ is a methodology developed by Arcus Compliance to both simplify and optimise the compliance process for small, medium and large businesses in the vape industry. Although CORE Compliance was designed with the European regulations in mind, its principles apply to anyone that is manufacturing a vape product and marketing that product anywhere in the world.

In essence, the principles of CORE Compliance represent good manufacturing practice (GMP), which is adopted all around the world under EU directives 2003/94/EC and in the USA under the FDA CFR (Food and Drug Administration Code of Federal Regulations) Parts 210 and 211.

The ethos is to create a basic roadmap that follows the entire life cycle of vape products and helps you to create a virtual wall around your products in the form of a compliance strategy and supporting due diligence.

The background

In researching how the vape industry viewed compliance, I realised that there was a distinct scepticism towards compliance and suppliers of compliance services. Given my own experience gained within OEM manufacturing, retail, brand ownership, general management consulting and regulatory compliance, I couldn't argue with this sentiment, but I knew that, nevertheless, regulatory compliance was a fact of life and the industry needed to up its game and find a way to meet the ever-increasing requirements that it would face.

The need for an overarching compliance strategy that included product stewardship and access to best practices from the pharmaceutical and tobacco industries was essential. In the absence of a specified global standard, I set about reviewing the basics of GMP, as well as other international quality management systems. I looked at risk assessment processes, scorecards, labelling and packaging regulations, consumer safety requirements, analytical requirements and everything else.

This research led me to the conclusion that my methodology needed to be a simple framework that considered all the regulations that impacted the vape industry and needed to work across all regions, not just in Europe. Given that, in general, the vape industry lacks the skills and experience to manage its own quality and regulatory affairs, it needed to be easy to apply and use.

It needed to focus on key areas of the product lifecycle – from inception to testing and all the way through to consumer safety. Using the European TPD and the European Environment Agency's data dictionary (https://circabc.europa.eu) as a base, I cross-referenced the requirements of other industry regulations and the basic needs of a vape manufacturer to create the CORE Compliance methodology.

The six key areas

CORE Compliance applies to six key areas of regulatory compliance, which are present in all regulatory frameworks in Europe and North America. These are:

1. Product data

2. Analytical data

3. Risk management

4. Quality management

5. Classification, labelling and packaging

6. Consumer safety and post-market surveillance

I felt that if we could create a system that addressed these key areas in a cost-efficient manner, then we could help you and the 3000+ other entrepreneurial micro-brands that steer our industry to compete with Big Tobacco – at least from a compliance perspective!

In Part 2, we will consider each of these key areas in turn and demonstrate how the CORE Compliance methodology can be applied to them. First, though, let's take a look at the methodology itself.

The methodology

The CORE Compliance methodology is broken down into four stages, constituting a series of simple processes that allow you to identify risk and then mitigate it:

1. **Control**

2. **Observe**

3. **React**

4. **Establish**

We begin by establishing your current compliant status (or not, as the case may be) (Control), then we review the data (Observe), build a compliance strategy based on the data (React) and finally implement the strategy (Establish).

By following these stages, you can easily identify and focus on your weaknesses without getting caught up in areas that you are already strong in. You then simplify your obligations and build robust due diligence, step by step. This staged process also allows you to implement much of the work inhouse or using low-cost Software as a Service (SaaS) tools, without high consultancy costs.

In following these four stages, you will not only be ring-fencing your products with proven processes, but also setting them apart from your nearest competitor and positioning yourself into the top league of brands that will still be around five years from now.

Stage 1: Control

The first stage of the methodology begins with a 'gap analysis'. To this end, we have devised a CORE Compliance Health Check. This is a scorecard system we have developed that allows you to get an idea of where you currently sit from a product stewardship and compliance perspective. It's entirely free and can be completed on our website: https://arcuscompliance.com/health-check

There are a possible sixty-four questions, covering the six key areas listed above. These are designed to extract all the necessary information, depending on your product type and level of compliance at that moment. Essentially, the questions reveal how well you understand the risks that might impact your products or your company, what processes you have in place to mitigate those risks and how committed you are to quality management, risk minimisation and consumer safety.

For example, in the product data section, you will enter the country or countries into which you are selling your products. You may be selling into South Africa, which is currently an unregulated market, so there is no need for a regulatory filing, but there may be some requirements for adherence to electrical safety regulations and general consumer safety obligations, so you will still need to produce the correct product data and documentation, appropriate packaging, and so on in compliance with local laws and regulations – and, of course, in the local language(s).

Or you may be selling zero-nicotine products (shortfills), which are officially classed as an unregulated product in certain countries, but, as in the example above, will still be subject to certain rules and regulations.

The size of your company will also determine how the competent authorities treat you. In Europe, for example, the authorities want to know whether your business is classified as an SME, as opposed to a multinational. Whereas a multinational would be expected to have a strong understanding of the regulations, the same might not be true of an SME. For this reason, there is some leniency in the application of regulations to smaller companies, but there is still a need for them to comply.

In other words, understanding the market and the product and business type is key to knowing what regulations are going to impact you and your products.

Once you have completed the Health Check, you will receive a bespoke thirty-plus page report that scores you on each aspect of your compliance strategy and identifies areas for improvement. This is the first step in your journey to building a robust due diligence process around your products.

Stage 2: Observe

On the basis of your Health Check report, you can begin to review your current position and identify the major gaps and risks that are present within your regulatory affairs and product stewardship processes. The report will enable you to quickly find faults (both large and small), establish the levels of the risks you have identified and prioritise which gaps need to be addressed first.

One essential ingredient of small businesses' strategies – and the focus of this book – that is often absent is risk management: an adverse effects system to control any safety concerns that may arise over your product. It is something they may not even have considered and, for this reason, may need specialist help in developing.

For example, Recital 45 of the TPD requires that 'manufacturers, importers, and distributors operate an appropriately robust system for the monitoring and recording of suspected adverse effects and inform the competent authorities about such effects so that appropriate action can be taken'.[2]

The key word here is 'appropriately'. The rule of thumb that we apply is: if you had a batch failure that affected 10% of your sales, would your system be able to cope with that many inquiries? For example, if you are selling batches of 10,000 units in the UK and you have a failure that affects 10% of a batch so that you receive 1,000 complaints or safety enquiries, your internal system needs to be capable of handling those 1,000 enquiries.

You could argue that a telephone number within your contraindications leaflet and an Excel spreadsheet to log the calls in is 'adequately robust', that you have enough staff to answer the phone (in English), record

---

2   TPD (Recital 45, p7), https://health.ec.europa.eu/system/ files/2016-11/dir_201440_en_0.pdf

adverse effects and customer data and report that to the competent authorities. However, if you are selling a million units per month into France, Germany and Spain, your system needs to be able to handle 100,000 enquiries in French, German and Spanish. And you will be required to demonstrate that. If the competent authorities don't believe you, you might end up arguing that claim in court – which could be costly in more ways than one.

Stage 3: React

Once you have completed the observation review, you can start creating a product stewardship and compliance strategy and building the documentation required to bridge the gaps in your ring-fence and mitigate the risks to your business, or you can engage specialists to do this for you.

Your strategy should have a focused timeline for improvement. It should be a feasible implementation plan and prioritise crucial procedural needs over 'nice to have' elements.

Stage 4: Establish

Finally, you will look at your resources and implement the strategy plan in order of priority and in line with your retained service contract. The implementation usually takes six to twelve months, depending on various factors. It will cover all applicable regulations and build your due diligence processes with regard to both downstream users and competent authorities.

Two essential elements for compliance

As well as the specialist advice and help explained above, there are two essential things that you will need to begin this journey towards robust compliance:

1. A cloud-based repository

Data integrity and visibility are important to every aspect of supply management. Having a centrally located database of supplier information and the required documentation will not only increase efficiency, but can also help you to maintain compliance.

If your data is held in multiple systems, or you are working with various business units, you will need a repository that accepts data from various sources and aggregates it to create the business intelligence needed, such as an interactive portal that allows suppliers to log in and enter details themselves. I have found that Google Drive works effectively for this need. You will also need a single point of contact (see Chapter 7).

2. A passion for the welfare of the industry

If you are in the vapour business to make as much cash as possible before the regulations catch up with you, the CORE Compliance methodology (and this book as a whole) will not be for you (and I wish you well on your journey). If, on the other hand, you are planning to create a stable brand that is recognised by the industry and is a market leader in quality, safe products, then CORE Compliance is essential.

Beyond that, it should be your aim (as it certainly is mine) to keep the vape industry 'boutique' for as long as possible. By ensuring that our compliance is 'adequately robust', we can maintain growth and ensure that independence and variety remain within an industry that has traditionally been controlled by Big Tobacco.

Summary

- CORE Compliance™ is a robust product stewardship and regulatory compliance methodology designed by Arcus Compliance Ltd.

- The methodology was developed by drawing from experience gained in various parts of the manufacturing chain of the vape industry.

- The methodology focuses on six key areas of regulatory compliance (worldwide): product data, analytical data, risk management, quality management, labelling and packaging and consumer safety.

- It comprises four stages: Control, Observe, React, Establish.

- The CORE methodology shares current best practices with even the smallest of micro-brands and allows you to keep the pressure on the big boys.

PART TWO
CORE COMPLIANCE IN ACTION

In this part of the book, I explain how to put CORE Compliance into action. I will elaborate on what you need to be controlling, what you need to observe, what you need to react to and then how you establish that. To do this, I will focus on the six areas that I have identified as being fundamental to a brand's regulatory compliance: product data, analytical data, risk management, quality management, labelling and packaging and consumer safety.

In each case, you should assess your current processes (Control), identify any gaps or potential weaknesses in them (Observe), address those gaps and weaknesses (React) and develop robust systems going forwards (Establish).

The information in the following chapters is based on our knowledge of best practice taken from working with a hundred-plus of the largest flavour brands in the industry. Each factor that needs to be addressed in each of the six areas is straightforward and non-technical. The essential thing is that they must all be subject to quality management processes, so that you will not only be sure of being compliant, but also be seen to be compliant.

FOUR
Product Data

It is debatable whether product data is the most important aspect of regulatory compliance but, certainly from my perspective, everything *starts* with the product and how you build it. Although convention might suggest that you address your overall risk assessment first, I believe that the single most important thing you can do is to get your product engineering processes in order.

The foundation of vape products is the flavour engineering stage, where robust CORE processes (Control, Observe, React, Establish) will ensure that you work only with pre-screened suppliers and use appropriately safe components.

This chapter will give you tools and processes that will make sure you know how to choose your flavour partners, build due diligence and make your product safe for your consumers.

Supplier due diligence

How much do you know about your flavour house?

Undertaking any level of due diligence on flavour house partners is almost unheard of, with the exception of some of the larger brands in the industry, but it is probably one of the most important decisions you could make.

Making a decision on a flavour house partner without ensuring, for example, that they will provide you with the required CAS numbers for the concentrates they are supplying or without asking them whether they are actually screening their concentrates for known banned substances is tantamount to playing Russian roulette.

In a regulated environment, it is essential to mitigate risk exposure, and the global nature of the vape industry means that we must follow a due diligence process when appointing any new third-party supplier. Put simply, this involves making appropriate enquiries to determine whether a supplier meets a specified set of benchmarks to ensure compliance.

By using a template for appointing a new supplier, you take the pain out of the process. Such a template should include the following points:

1. Trust, but verify

Don't assume that simply because Major Brand A uses Flavour House B that Flavour House B will also be right for you. The fact that the market leader is using them doesn't necessarily mean that they have actually done any due diligence on the supplier. Don't be a sheep. Do your own research to make sure that the products you are putting out there are suitable for a regulated market.

Don't believe everything you hear or are told, either; verify it rather than accepting it as fact. Reach out to any current or previous clients of the supplier and see what they have to say about them. See if you can validate any testimonials that the supplier has on their website. If they have none then ask for some and follow them up to validate them.

You may, of course, find that it isn't possible to verify everything and, in the end, you may have to 'go with your gut', but having a process and keeping evidence of your efforts will demonstrate due diligence.

2. Supplier status

The first and most obvious check to make is whether the supplier is registered, eg, with Companies House. Ask questions like:

- When was the company incorporated?

- Who owns it?

- Does it have a registered office?

- Is it registered for VAT?

- Does it have product liability insurance?

- What quality management systems (QMS) does it have in place?

Verifying that the supplier is financially solvent is obviously essential. Using a commercial credit check agency is advisable if this is within your budget, but don't forget to also speak to your contacts in the industry to find out what their experiences have been with this supplier (or others).

A trade association membership is usually a good indication that the supplier takes their business and industry seriously and is reliable, so ask what trade associations the supplier is a member of and verify that membership with the trade body.

By the way, if you are not already a member of a trade association yourself, it is worth considering joining. Membership gives you a 'voice', access to lobbying, advice on best practices, as well as networking opportunities. Membership will also give your business credibility.

3. Manufacturers or blenders?

There are essentially two types of concentrate suppliers – Tier 1 and Tier 2 – and which you buy from can have significant consequences for your compliance process.

A Tier 1 supplier is one that manufactures from raw materials. These are generally the 'big guys' who are bulk-buying raw materials. They have their own inhouse flavour team and flavourists developing flavours unique to them and marketing them as 'the best available'. If you're buying flavours from a Tier 1 supplier, they will normally provide you with the data you need to make a regulatory filing with the competent authorities (see Chemical identity disclosure below).

A Tier 2 supplier, on the other hand, will use finished concentrates produced by Tier 1 suppliers, buying, say, a strawberry from one and a blackberry from another, mixing them together and creating something that they think is unique and marketing it as their own. The problem is that the Tier 1 flavour houses won't normally give their 'secret recipes' to the Tier 2 house, which is, in a sense, their competitor, in case the latter buys the raw materials and makes it themselves, thereby cutting out the Tier 1 supplier.

So, if you are buying from a Tier 2 flavour house, you might not be able to get the data you need to make a regulatory filing with the competent authorities. If you don't obtain these data and are asked for them by a competent authority, you will be back to the drawing board (ie, needing to reformulate that product to be able to sell it).

Generally, however, while a flavour house will not release CAS data directly to you as the client, it will to a third party that is handling your regulatory compliance for you (a compliance partner). The disclosure is usually done under a non-disclosure agreement, which may include a clause that the data can only be released to an official body such as the EU Commission.

4. Chemical identity disclosure

In the US, the FDA has created a system that requires flavour houses to submit details of the formulation of their concentrates, which are then given specific codes, so that e-liquid manufacturers can use these codes in their submissions. For example, they might declare that their product comprises 5% of strawberry code XYZ and 15% of blackcurrant code ABC, etc.

The EU system, on the other hand, requires manufacturers to submit a full recipe listing and their percentage inclusion in the final formula with the relevant chemical identity data, which normally consists of CAS numbers.

This means that part of your flavour house due diligence process is to request a full written CAS disclosure: ie, a set of unique reference numbers identifying each chemical included in a liquid. This is something very few brand owners do in advance of building a concentrate into their e-liquid, but it is absolutely fundamental; failing to do so can derail your entire regulatory compliance strategy (in Europe, at least).

While it is possible to make a TPD notification without CAS numbers through the EU's Common Entry Gate system, it does inhibit your ability to rate the hazardous status of your e-liquid (and, therefore, to obtain a CLP classification) or obtain toxicological studies (see Chapter 5). This, in turn, impacts various other elements, such as your safety data sheet (see Chapter 8).

As explained above, your supplier may be unable, or unwilling, to provide such data (while there are some very professional flavour houses, there are others that simply won't provide a CAS disclosure), so it is essential that you have established from day one whether that supplier is going to provide you with CAS data. This can be done by simply emailing the flavour house prior to the sampling stage and asking them for details of their processes for releasing CAS data.

This simple step will act as a filter to help you find the most professional flavour house partners and add to the credibility of your due diligence processes. By establishing this in advance, you can also save yourself an awful lot of stress in the long run. We have had clients come to us that have had to completely reformulate their best flavours because a flavour house wouldn't release CAS to them when required.

There are allowances for the protection of intellectual property with certain member states in the EU, although these vary from member state to member state. For notification purposes, any chemical comprising 0.1% or less of the final recipe can be grouped under a generic heading, such as 'Strawberry Flavour' or 'Apple Flavour'. Some flavour houses take this as an excuse to withhold CAS data, without taking into account that the specific chemical they have chosen to withhold could be present in other elements of the recipe, which could take it above the 0.1% threshold. For this reason, it is essential that you obtain full disclosure of all chemical identities from your flavour house partner.

If there is no CAS number for a particular chemical (because it is a natural flavouring, for example), a FEMA number, Additive number, FL number, EC number or Other number must be indicated (in that order of preference):

- A CAS number is the preferred identifier and is used globally.

- FEMA is the Flavor and Extract Manufacturers Association.

- An Additive of 'E' number is relevant if the ingredient is a food additive. E numbers are set out in Annexes II and III to Regulation (EC) 1333/2008.

- The FL number or European Flavouring number relates to Annex I to Regulation (EC) 1334/2008.

- The EC or European Community number is a unique seven-digit identifier assigned to substances for regulatory purposes within the EU by the European Commission.

- An 'Other number' is an ID number allocated by the submitter in the absence of any of the above-listed number types. This could be a catalogue number from the flavour house or an internal number.

In summary, you can proceed if you don't have CAS data, but it makes assembling your overall regulatory requirements much more difficult.

Aggregated CAS presentation

In simple terms, an aggregated CAS presentation is an expanded or exploded version of your recipe. So, rather than showing a flavour concentrate at a certain percentage, it shows a chemical identity at a certain percentage.

An aggregated CAS presentation is the cornerstone of your product stewardship and allows you to screen for banned substances, source toxicological studies, compile safety data sheets and, crucially, sign a declaration of conformity with confidence. Having the ability to identify banned substances at an early stage and make adjustments is key, and creating an aggregated CAS presentation for each of your recipes will not only provide robust due diligence, but also make each of the next steps in your compliance process easier.

Ingredient purity data

Most regulations or directives will have some sort of requirement for you to use the highest purity ingredients. For example, if you are using a carrier liquid such as propylene glycol or vegetable glycerin, the competent authorities will want to see certificates of analysis that demonstrate that these carriers are safe for human consumption – whether that is pharmaceutical grade or food grade.

Ultimately, the responsibility for ensuring ingredient purity falls on the brand owner and manufacturer, but how do you assess the purity of all your ingredients? While some flavour houses will remove any known banned substances, they might not, for example, run a toxicological risk assessment (see Chapter 5) on their products on the basis of them being inhaled.

The system that you employ in order to determine ingredient purity does not need to be complex; it can simply be a set of basic processes based on supplier testing, location, price, availability, etc. However, you must document this system as part of your due diligence process.

My suggestion is that you write a formal request to your supplier (or intended supplier) asking for all testing certificates, certificates of origin and anything else they can provide you with. Keep all these documents and ensure that they are updated as newer versions of your flavours are released.

Green & white lists

Green lists are lists of chemicals that do not contain any known banned substances, ie, are deemed to be safe for human consumption. (The TPD, for example, directs that e-liquids must not contain any ingredients that 'pose a risk to human health in heated or unheated form' and specifies nine chemicals that are not allowed to be in vapour products.)[3]

I use the term 'deemed' to be safe, as a green list may still allow harmful chemicals to find their way into vape liquids. As we have seen, many (Tier 2) flavour houses purchase concentrates from the larger (Tier 1) houses and blend them to create a new flavour, but they have no technical ability when it comes to the intricacies of reformulating. Although they may make the effort to screen them and remove known banned substances such as diacetyl and acetyl propionyl, they don't always dig any deeper and remove all carcinogens and respiratory sensitisers from their concentrates.

Nevertheless, a flavour house green list is an excellent starting point towards ensuring that you are using 'safe' concentrates and not generic concentrates such as those prevalent in the US market. If your (prospective) flavour house does not have a green list and has no intention of creating one, it's a warning that you need to change suppliers.

A white list, on the other hand, is an exclusive list of chemicals that are allowed to be in vapour products; in other words, any chemical not on a white list cannot be included. (Most Middle East countries, for example, have white lists rather than green lists.)

---

3   TPD (page 27), https://health.ec.europa.eu/system/files/2016-11/dir_201440_en_0.pdf

Although working to a white list (as opposed to a green list) makes your life simpler, in practice, due diligence must still be carried out. In other words, you must still test everything to make sure that the combination of chemicals doesn't produce anything potentially harmful.

Dependency ratio

Another important part of your product data review is to list all the flavour houses you are working with, along with the number of concentrates from each flavour house you are using in your recipes, so that you can calculate how many or which of your flavours are bringing in the most revenue. This will tell you how dependent your business is on a particular flavour house and/or flavour concentrate.

The reason this is so important is that high dependency on one flavour house or, worse, a single flavour concentrate, means high risk to your business. Ask yourself: What would happen if a key component of my bestselling e-liquid was discontinued?

We have had clients with ten or twenty flavours in their portfolio, but one or two of them are accounting for 60, 70 or even 80% of their revenue. This means that if the flavour house should discontinue that particular product for any reason, the client suddenly faces a massive drop in revenue.

It could be that your products have a 'secret ingredient' or 'X factor' that gives them an edge over everything else on the market; and this may be a single ingredient that is used in a tiny quantity but is, nevertheless, central to your marketing and sales strategy. Without it, you lose your competitive advantage.

So, it is essential to identify (Observe) how reliant you are on a particular concentrate or flavour house and, if necessary, build a continuity agreement to protect your business from the unexpected discontinuation of that ingredient or supplier (React).

Continuity agreement

A continuity agreement provides you with a safety net in case a supplier goes out of business, their business is bought out, or they simply decide to discontinue a particular flavour concentrate. In signing the agreement, they undertake to continue providing the product for a certain period (eg, three or six months) or an agreed-upon period for you to either stock up or have time to reformulate your product.

A continuity agreement can be a specific agreement, or simply a clause within a supply agreement. There are various forms it can take, from agreed time periods based on volume purchased, to predetermined minimum notice periods for phasing-out. If you are a major customer, they may even agree to provide you with the formulas in the event of closure (whether through purchase or licence) so that you can get them made elsewhere.

One of our clients had a unique flavour that was selling several hundred thousand bottles per month... until their supplier discontinued a key component of it without warning. The client had enough stock to last a maximum of three months, but no plan beyond that – and no continuity agreement. It was the beginning of a very stressful period of frantic reformulations and a very uncertain outcome – stress that could have been avoided with a little forethought and product stewardship planning. Having a continuity agreement in place can save you not only worry and uncertainty, but also an awful lot of time and money in the long run.

Depending on the volume you are purchasing, you may get some resistance to your request for a continuity agreement, in which case you will need to decide whether you move forward with the flavour house or look for another supplier.

Product engineering

Product engineering means creating a standardised process for creating a new e-liquid. As it is essentially a creative process, there is no set method and each brand has its own methodology. Nevertheless, it is certainly essential to instil a level of quality management into the process.

It is basically a question of writing down and recording each step in the process so that it is easily replicable and you are doing it in the same methodical way every time. This will not only minimise your risk of something going wrong, but also further strengthen your due diligence strategy. Product engineering can be broken down into the following steps:

1. Standardised recipe format

The first step is to establish a standardised recipe format. Again, there is no right or wrong way of doing this, and it will certainly be iterative. You might find that you have started in a particular way, but this isn't working the right way, so you change it. The important thing is to update your processes each time and record it as an 'improved version' (Control).

For example, you might have columns on an Excel spreadsheet headed 'Flavour house A: strawberry, 5%. Flavour house B: banana, 3%. Flavour house C: strawberry, 2%.' The next columns would contain details of those three concentrates with, ideally, their CAS numbers, with the percentage inclusion of each.

Then, if you do decide to reformulate, you are able to pinpoint the elements that might be changed rather than hunting for that envelope or napkin you scribbled the original formula on... Which leads us to the second step.

2. Version control

In a high-pressure environment where things are changing very quickly, you need to make sure that your system is able to record precisely when you change a recipe, how and why, so that if in three years' time you realise that a reformulation isn't as good as you thought it was and want to change it again, you can see exactly how and why it was changed. Was the change driven by new regulations, a problem with the recipe, availability of concentrates...? Too often we have seen cases where people cannot remember why or how something was changed because it wasn't properly recorded – or recorded at all.

There is also a compliance implication in this. If a competent authority should one day knock on your door and say, 'There's a problem with this product. What can you tell us about it?' you will be able to demonstrate, for example, that the 'problem' ingredient has not been in it since such-and-such a date, when it was changed for this other ingredient, which is clean. Once again, it is a question of due diligence and quality management – of applying the CORE Compliance process.

Raw materials or concentrates?

Although the majority of the vape businesses are using flavour concentrates that they purchase from flavour house partners, there is a growing movement among brands to formulate their own flavours using raw materials at a molecular level. This means that, rather than purchasing a 'strawberry' concentrate that could contain fifty-plus individual chemicals, you create your own strawberry flavour, using those same fifty-plus chemicals, but perhaps in a slightly different ratio.

This may not be something that you are able to do, for lack of appropriate resources, but it is possible to contract a professional flavourist on a project basis to do such reformulations for you. This method is extremely cost-effective and ultimately gives you complete ownership of your recipes, which adds value to your company through the creation of intellectual property.

It also enables you to remove potential problem chemicals with surgical precision. Imagine the headache of being told that your chosen 'strawberry' concentrate has a known carcinogen in its make-up and the flavour house won't do anything about it... Now imagine that you have built your concentrate from raw materials and you know that this carcinogen is called furfural. It becomes infinitely easier to target that one chemical, find a replacement and remove the risk.

Recipe screening

As we have seen, using a green list to build your e-liquids is a positive step, but it doesn't guarantee that you will have a clean and safe final product. Further work must be done to screen the recipe to ensure that it is safe and to create a complete toxicological risk assessment (see Chapter 5).

The TPD requires that all your concentrates and final recipes be screened for chemicals known to be carcinogenic, mutagenic or toxic for reproduction (or reprotoxic), known as CMRs. Many smaller manufacturers may not do this themselves, but rely on the flavour houses to do it for them. However, not all flavour houses will do so; instead, they may simply take the baseline information from the TPD and say, 'Those nine banned substances are not in it, so the recipe is fine.' This may not be enough, so it is really up to you to ensure that your recipes are properly screened.

There are more than 700 chemicals in e-liquid manufacture that fall into the various categories highlighted by the European authorities as harmful to human health. Many of these are present in flavour house concentrates, so it is essential that you take this step to verify the safety of your product and ensure that due diligence has been conducted. There are tools available to help you screen your recipes (see Further Resources at the back of the book).

Final aggregated recipe file

The final step in your product data compliance process is preparing an aggregated and deduplicated CAS presentation, which can be a complex exercise. If, for example, a product contains four concentrates, each of which contains up to fifty chemicals, there could be up to 200 chemicals to be included in your file. However, there is every likelihood that a number of those chemicals are duplicated across the four concentrates, so they must be deduplicated and the final percentage inclusion in the recipe adjusted accordingly.

This process will reveal the chemicals that constitute more than 0.1% of a product and must, therefore, be declared. If you don't go through the deduplication process, you can be misled into thinking that a chemical is below the 0.1% threshold when, in fact, it is above the threshold in total and must be declared.

It also has a bearing on your CLP classification (see Chapter 8). The total hazardous content of a liquid will have an effect on the pictograms and what warnings must be shown on the labelling (which we'll look at in Chapter 8).

Summary

- Regulatory compliance starts with the product. Every aspect of its construction must be monitored and recorded.

- Undertaking due diligence on flavour house partners is one of the most important things to do.

- Don't make assumptions or believe what you are told; carry out your own research in order to make sure that your products are suitable for a regulated market.

- Check a flavour house's company status and trade association membership.

- Are your flavour houses' manufacturers or blenders, and can (or will) they supply a full written CAS disclosure?

- Responsibility for ensuring the purity of your ingredients rests with you.

- Green lists (chemicals that do not contain any known banned substances) and white lists (chemicals that are allowed to be in vapour products) are a useful starting point, but don't guarantee that you will have a clean and safe final product; further screening is required.

- High dependency on one flavour house, or worse, a single flavour concentrate, means high risk to your business.

- A continuity agreement provides you with a safety net in case a supplier goes out of business, they are bought out or they decide to discontinue a particular concentrate.

- Product engineering means creating a standardised process for creating a new e-liquid, ie, a standardised recipe format and version control (when, how and why things have been changed).

- The final step in your product data compliance process is preparing an aggregated and deduplicated CAS presentation.

FIVE

Analytical Data

This chapter will show you how to apply the CORE Compliance process in compiling the required data to comply with a variety of regulations, including test results, toxicological studies and dosage consistency.

As you may need lab partners to carry out the necessary testing, we begin with some dos and don'ts of choosing a lab partner.

Lab partner due diligence

The temptation for most manufacturers is to choose a lab partner on the basis of price, but going with the cheapest option has been proven to cost much more in the long run. There is an abundance of labs popping up and offering low-cost tests for the vaping industry, but on closer inspection, many of them turn out to be affiliated to or owned by retail chains or vape brands. This not only begs the question whether you want a potential competitor knowing your analytical results, but also whether they have the competence to test e-liquids.

If a laboratory is a subsidiary of a tobacco company, for example, it might use methodologies and equipment designed for tobacco testing, not vape products and e-liquids, so that their results might not be as accurate on vape products. Even government-contracted laboratories tend to have set methods, whereas you need a lab to work with you and your product to obtain the most accurate result. Certain CBD products, for example, can yield wildly different results depending on the testing method used.

I recommend that you work with an established independent lab that has a 'pedigree' in vape products testing. The key credential to look for – in fact, a lot of regulations require it – is ISO 17025 accreditation. This means that an approved body has looked at their methodologies and their QMS and that the certificate you get at the end of the testing process is valid.

Beyond that, you need to decide whether a lab's methods will be appropriate for you. Is their way of testing going to get the best results for your product? Will they run, say, just two samples through the machine when you want them to test nine samples? Although often more expensive, an independent lab will be more willing to adapt their methods in order to obtain the most accurate results for your products.

As well as cost, time is a consideration. Simple, high-throughput tests are quick to run, but there may be a trade-off with the quality of the end data.

Testing methodologies

As with lab partners, although the EU doesn't currently require international standards to be met, you should ensure that a lab's testing methodologies have been third-party-validated, because this means that the results are accurate, repeatable and not subject to unacceptable deviation. Validation is ensured by an ISO 17025 accreditation, or can be carried out by a body such as the United Kingdom Accreditation Service (UKAS).

Once again, this should be part of your due diligence process, so if anything goes wrong and there is an investigation, you will be seen to be doing everything you possibly can to ensure that your products are safe.

Toxicological risk assessments

Toxicological risk assessments are currently not required by legislation, but if something should go wrong and one of your products causes harm to consumers, you could face criminal proceedings if the authorities deem that you haven't done enough to ensure that the product was safe. If, on the other hand, you have carried out a full toxicological risk assessment as part of your regulatory submission, this will demonstrate that you have exercised due diligence. It will also, of course, reduce the risk of something going wrong.

A toxicological risk assessment must be carried out by a qualified person – usually a graduate from a school of pharmacy or someone with a postgraduate qualification in toxicology. Otherwise, the assessment might be rejected by the competent authority.

It is also important for you to instruct the toxicologist as to exactly what it is they are assessing. In the case of a vape product, you don't want a toxicology assessment that is solely focused on its CBD content. It should also assess whether the product contains irritants or is it likely to cause reactions. They need to look at the product as a whole, ie, at how its components interact, whereas cheaper, off-the-shelf assessment methods might only look at the individual components in isolation.

If a toxicological risk assessment concludes that the product data are insufficient, you will need to undertake a toxicological study.

Toxicological studies

A toxicological study is a clinical process undertaken in a lab. As with toxicological risk assessments, studies are mostly carried out by specialist companies.

There are essentially two types of toxicological study: in vitro and in silico. An in vitro test involves physically dropping tiny amounts of a chemical or compound into a testing dish and studying the reactions that take place and then changing the environment to see whether the reactions change – for which a 'person in a white lab coat' is required.

An in silico test is a computer-based study where the characteristics of the chemical or compound are input into a computer model or algorithm, which predicts, on the basis of certain factors, whether the chemical or compound will be toxic.

With animal testing being viewed as a last option, in silicon testing can help to narrow down the scope of animal studies, thus reducing cost, both financial as well as ethical.

Once you have the required data, you will feed this back into a new toxicological risk assessment. In that sense, it is a continual process: if, at any point, you change any ingredient or substance in the product, or if the flavour house changes the specification of a concentrate it contains, you must re-run your toxicological risk assessment to determine whether the change affects the outcome – ie, the safety of the product.

There are two things to consider in relation to toxicological studies: cost and time – both of which can be considerable. The good news is that under the current TPD, competent authorities in the EU are accepting a toxicological monograph in place of a toxicological study. This is essentially a 'library search' of studies that have already been conducted on a specific chemical or CAS number. Once you have done this, you can work with a toxicologist to produce an overall assessment of the recipe, which is a lot cheaper than conducting a full toxicological study.

Nicotine dosage consistency

It is obviously important that your product delivers a consistent dosage of nicotine. This can be tested using a so-called 'puff machine'. Originally designed for the tobacco industry, puff machines draw on a cigarette at set intervals over a set time. Most of them can be modified so that they draw on e-cigarettes.

Nicotine-per-puff testing

Even more important than dosage consistency is that your product actually delivers the amount of nicotine per puff that you claim it does. This is much simpler to calculate and can be done mathematically. You simply divide the amount of nicotine by the number of puffs to get the nicotine-per-puff figure. Say your product holds 10ml of e-liquid at a strength of 20mg. This equals a 200mg total nicotine content in the bottle. If we assume that a user gets approximately 1,500 puffs from the 10ml bottle, 200 x 1,500 = 0.133mg or 133ug per puff (3ml) of e-liquid, containing 30mg of nicotine, and it gives you 30 puffs.

The first thing to verify is that the product does actually hold 10ml of liquid and that there are actually 200mg of nicotine in those 10ml of liquid.

The question then arises, however: How big is a puff? No two people's puffs will be exactly the same 'size', and the variation can be considerable. How do you accurately determine the amount of nicotine per puff? The answer is either to include in your declaration the puff size that your figures are based on, or to run several tests using different puff sizes and give an average figure – preferably along with the highest and lowest measurements. This will demonstrate due diligence and usually satisfy the authorities.

Emissions testing

Emissions testing is another thing that must be carried out by a specialised independent laboratory. There are essentially three things to test for: nicotine output, carbon compounds, and any banned flavour compounds.

First, you need to check that your product is outputting the amount of nicotine you say it does. This is obviously crucial, as the nicotine is what 'satisfies' the user.

Carbonyl compounds are created by thermal decomposition as the e-liquid is heated. The base liquids for any vape e-liquid are propylene glycol (PG) and vegetable glycerine (VG). When heated, they break down and produce compounds such as formaldehyde and acetaldehyde, which are carcinogenic. Therefore, the levels of these compounds must be within certain limits for the product to be deemed safe.

The third thing an emissions test must check for is the presence of any banned flavouring compounds that might have found their way into the product, such as diacetyl, which in the early 2000s was found to be associated with a disease that became known as 'popcorn lung'. Although in theory these will have been picked up at an earlier stage in the manufacturing process, testing for them at this point provides you with a double-check that the recipe is exactly as it should be – yet another example of due diligence.

Materials testing

Whereas an emissions test is concerned with the effects of heating the e-liquid in a vape product, materials testing focuses on the effects of heating the product's other components. These include any metals (eg, a stainless steel heating coil), cotton (used as a wicking material) and silicon (used to make the seals in the pot or tank).

For example, if you use certain low-grade cottons to make your wicks, there is a chance that, when they are heated, they will produce arsenic. When combined with oxygen, silicon produces silicates which can be harmful when inhaled, so testing must demonstrate that no silicate particles are coming off the silicon seals in your product – particularly if it is a disposable or pod device where the coil and wiring pass through a seal.

Another potentially harmful substance to check for is lead. If low-quality solder has been used to make a metal tank, for example, this may emit small quantities of lead.

There are published methods for these kinds of tests, but, again, you will probably need to commission a laboratory to carry them out for you.

Flavourings

If you are using natural fruit- or tobacco-flavoured e-liquids, these will also need to be tested for potentially harmful substances. Tobacco is notorious for attracting pests, so plants are often sprayed with pesticides, as, of course, are fruit trees. There may also be traces of solvents used to extract the oil from tobacco leaves.

You should ask your supplier to provide results of any testing they have done. Any reputable supplier will be happy to supply certification from the extraction company confirming that appropriate testing has been carried out. If you are championing natural flavourings, ensure that you have traceability all down the supply chain and can show that they have been properly processed. This is part of your due diligence process.

Although they have a poor reputation, from a toxicological perspective, artificial flavourings are much less likely to be contaminated than natural flavourings, because the regulations that apply to them are so much tighter. Artificial flavourings are also more predictable than natural flavourings, as they have been produced in a clean room, with calculated and calibrated scales and mixing regimes, whereas natural products are subject to variation and unexpected contamination.

Stability testing

The stability of your product is related to its shelf life. For example, if you fill your products with 20mg of e-liquid, will they still contain 20mg in six months' time? And will the flavour still be the same as when the liquid was mixed?

Flavours can react and interact over time. Because of their acid content, for example, citrus flavourings can degrade the nicotine content in a liquid.

The only way to find out whether such degradation will occur is to conduct a stability test. The standard test is a twelve-month study; it is possible to conduct an accelerated test, but this is obviously less reliable and more of an estimate. If you have a product that is prone to rapid degradation, you might want monthly test results.

Most labs apply the pharmaceutical standard, which is 10% deviation. This means that if your product is 20mg, it is deemed to be out of spec once it has lost 2mg. This will determine its shelf life.

For some markets, including the US, UAE and New Zealand, stability testing is required by law and it must be conducted by an ISO 17025-accredited laboratory. The EU is currently less strict about stability testing, and you may be able to simply use the standard shelf life given to you by the nicotine manufacturers. However, the MHRA has recently been looking at tightening its testing regulations, so you may be asked to justify the shelf life indicated on your product packaging. Although it isn't compulsory, this means that, realistically, there is no way for you to be able to produce concrete data to support a shelf life without doing a stability study.

Leachables and extractables

Another requirement in some countries (the US, for example) is that your product be tested for leachables and extractables.

'Leachables' refers to the potential for, say, a plastic container to leach any harmful substances into the e-liquid inside it. 'Extractables' refers to potentially harmful effects of environmental stress on the product or its packaging. This might include direct sunlight or extreme temperatures that cause a reaction in the e-liquid.

Testing for leachables and extractables doesn't have to be done in a laboratory. If you are using a plastic container, for example, the plastic is likely already to have been tested, so all you need to do is find and refer to the relevant study or studies. Alternatively, testing for leachables and extractables can be combined with, say, stability testing, which could save you money.

Summary

- You will need to compile and produce certain analytical data to comply with a variety of regulations, depending on the country or countries you are selling into.

- You will need to commission a lab partner for most of these data.

- Resist the temptation to choose a lab partner on the basis of price, which can cost you far more in the long run.

- Ensure that a lab's testing methodologies have been third-party-validated.

- If you decide to include toxicological risk assessments as part of your regulatory submission, these must be done by a qualified person.

- If a toxicological risk assessment finds that the product data are insufficient, you will need to undertake a toxicological study.

- If you change any ingredient or substance in the product, or if the flavour house changes the specification of a concentrate it contains, you must re-run your toxicological risk assessment.

- Your product must be shown to deliver a consistent dosage of nicotine, as well as the amount of nicotine per puff that you claim it does.

- You must also test for potentially harmful carbon compounds and any banned flavour compounds.

- Materials such as metals, cotton and silicon in your product should be tested to ensure that harmful substances do not contaminate the e-liquid.

- If you are using natural fruit- or tobacco-flavoured e-liquids (as opposed to artificial flavourings), these also need to be tested for potentially harmful substances.

- The stability of your product (ie, its shelf life) should be tested or otherwise verifiable.

- For some markets, your product should also be tested for leachables and extractables.

SIX
Quality Management

W hen submitting a notification via the EU-CEG, you are required to make six quality and safety declarations for your product. In other words, you must undertake to provide proof, if required, that your products are fit for purpose and safe for the consumer to use.

It should be noted in this respect that, although the regulations specify *what* is required, they don't detail *how* those requirements are to be met. This is up to you to determine.

The simplest way to ensure that you are meeting all the requirements and that an inspector won't come knocking at your door demanding evidence is to obtain ISO 9001 certification, but there are obviously cost (and time) implications to this, as will be explained.

By applying the CORE Compliance process, you can ensure that your products pass muster in the EU and other world markets.

QMS

As with production processes and emissions testing, the TPD doesn't stipulate an international standard for QMS, but it does require you to have a set of (written) processes which ensure that your product quality is consistent and replicable.

You can purchase a templated 'off-the-shelf' QMS system designed for generic manufacturing, which might cost between £2,000 and £5,000. Or, you can go to a consultant and commission a bespoke QMS, tailored to your business, which would be much more robust, for ten times this amount.

To save cost, you can use templates for generic operations (eg, your legal register – see below) and bespoke solutions for operations specific to the vape industry, but the industry is relatively new, so there are few applicable templates and most quality management processes will need to be written specifically for your business.

To sell your products in the UAE, however, you are required by the S5030 bill to have ISO 9001 for your manufacturing processes. For the US market, you must submit to the FDA a pre-market tobacco application (PMTA), for which an internationally approved QMS is required. As we have said, it is likely that the EU and other markets will follow suit in this respect.

The cost of obtaining ISO 9001 certification varies greatly depending both on the size of your business (eg, how many employees you have, how many sites and whether these are in different countries) and the consultant implementing it. It can also be a protracted process: usually between six and twelve months.

Legal register

The first thing a QMS should do is enable you to identify any regulations, standards or specifications that (might) apply to your product type in each of the countries you sell into. The list of these is your legal register, which in itself will demonstrate that you have applied a QMS and conducted due diligence with regard to regulatory compliance.

You should also ensure that you have a person in your company who is responsible for the legal register and regularly ensures that the company is in compliance with all the relevant legislation, etc. Make sure the register is dated each time it is checked so that there is a log of all your practices.

Technical file

A technical file (or dossier) is a document describing that you have systems in place to ensure a consistent manufacturing process. It should contain:

- Information relating to the way it is designed.

- How it is built.

- The relevant gas chromatography-mass spectrometry (GC-MS).

- Its labelling and packaging.

- How the product information is passed on to the consumer.

- How it is tested.

- How risks are assessed.

- How relevant requirements have been met.

In other words, everything to do with how that product has been manufactured and marketed. It should also include:

- A list of standards that have been applied.

- Test reports from your suppliers showing the standards that the product was tested to (eg, EN or IEC).

- The conformity assessment procedure applied to the product.

- A description of the control philosophy and logic.

- Quality control and commissioning procedures.

- Data sheets for critical sub-assemblies.

- A full parts list.

- A list of materials used.

- Any wiring and circuitry diagrams.

- Copies of any markings and labels.

- A copy of the instructions.

- User maintenance installation information.

- The CE or UKCA declaration of conformity (this is the most important).

A technical file is a EU requirement of manufacturers of electronic devices – any product needing a CE or UKCA mark (see Chapter 1) – and must be provided to any EU member state, or surveillance authority, if requested. Technical files must be retained for a minimum of ten years from the date on which the product is first and last placed on the UK or EU market.

If any of the above information is confidential, you should discuss this with your suppliers and ask them if they will provide the necessary documentation to a regulatory authority if requested.

In a sense, a technical file is an 'insurance document'. It is not passed to downstream users – whether wholesalers, distributors or retailers. It is only produced when requested either for a routine check, or when anything goes wrong at a local level and the enforcement body or the competent authority 'knocks on your door' and says, 'Show us what you've done to test the safety of this product.'

Without a technical file to show them, you could find yourself facing heavy penalties.

Batch recording

Article 20 of the TPD requires batch numbers to be printed on all your products. This is essentially for recall and surveillance purposes. For example, if you have sold batches A1–A5 to a company in Germany and they show up in the French market, you need to be able to demonstrate to the competent authority or the enforcement body that you have a system in place for identifying where your products are sold.

They will then go to the distributor or the primary customer in Germany and take action against them for selling it into a market that it is non-compliant with, rather than taking action against you as the manufacturer. In effect you are assisting the competent authorities to clamp down on the sale of stolen goods, illegal selling-on, counterfeiting and so on, as well as ensuring that you avoid the incalculable reputational damage that can result from a seizure of your products.

There is an increasing requirement for traceability of tobacco products. From 2023, all unit packets of cigarettes and loose tobacco must be marked with a unique identifier. It is possible that such regulations will be extended to vape products in due course. Having adequate batch numbering systems in place, including accurate recording of batch numbers and the initial customers of each batch, will help you to handle any investigation, as well as show that you are conducting due diligence as part of a robust compliance strategy.

It is always preferable to put such systems in place and be able to provide the required information in a timely and efficient manner than to have to scramble to collect the data, effectively shutting the gate after the horse has bolted. It is a lot cheaper to put a compliant product on the market than it is to take a non-compliant product off the market.

Batch testing

There is currently no requirement under the TPD for batches to be tested to the same standards as would be applied at the time of product notification (although such a requirement has recently been discussed and would be very simple to introduce). However, enforcement bodies and competent authorities do carry out sample testing: taking a product off the shelf and comparing its chemical make-up with what was submitted in the original notification.

In any case, batch testing is a very good way of ensuring that the quality of your products is consistent – that the quality you signed off on day one remains the same two, three or four years down the line. There are various reasons why something could go wrong with a particular batch, for example, an issue with the components, the concentrates or the carrying agents. These issues could be accidental or the result of an intentional change in the production process. Concentrate suppliers in certain countries (eg, China) are prone to cut corners by substituting different ingredients in order to save money, which ultimately affects the quality and/or safety of your products.

The only way to ensure that this isn't happening is to batch test, which involves comparing the GC-MS of different batches of the same product. If all the peaks and troughs on the chart match, you can be confident that the batches are consistent. If not, you will immediately see it and be able to identify what has gone wrong.

Regular batch testing is an essential part of your due diligence and regulatory compliance processes, particularly if you are outsourcing your manufacturing.

Traceability

Batch recording is one aspect of the wider issue of traceability: ensuring that everything you do is properly recorded so that, if need be, you can provide solid evidence of having acted in accordance with regulations or standards, or of having carried out due diligence in your processes.

We have seen many cases of businesses that didn't have adequate records and whose systems buckled under pressure from the authorities when something went wrong and investigations were initiated. Unfortunately, authorities are often also incompetent in such circumstances. The onus is on you to be competent for them, or their lack of competence can land you in deep trouble.

File structures

As soon as you store information in a computer system, a number of different issues arise due to the fact that the information will be accessible by multiple people, who may be able to change it, add to it, delete it or – worst of all – duplicate it so that different versions of the 'same' information are available simultaneously, causing confusion and, possibly, catastrophe.

This means that you need to look carefully at the file structures in your information technology to ensure that there is no duplication of information. If you put information into the cloud, for example, make sure that it is only in one place – a single 'place of truth'. This is more difficult than it sounds, as there are so many temptations for people to duplicate data – mainly because it is simple and convenient. If, for example, you are working on a document and are not sure if it is in the cloud (or other 'filing' system) already, it is a lot quicker to put it in there than to check whether it is there already.

Whenever you have a team collaborating on anything, ensure that you make it as convenient as possible for them to avoid duplication, and to store everything in a single 'place of truth'.

Version control

Another aspect of traceability is version control, which means keeping track of all iterations of, or changes to, a product or process – not only in case of checks or investigations by external authorities, but also in your own interests. This is so you can see where you have come from and how you have ended up where you are (especially if you need to go back to a previous stage in your development).

To use a simple metaphor: if you post a letter into a letterbox, you don't have that letter any more. Nor does anyone else. And there is no record that it ever existed. To prove it, you need to keep a copy of it, date and time-stamped. In other words, you need to have version control, which is basically a way of time-stamping a digital document.

Then, if you need to, you can go back to it at any point and say with 100% confidence, 'This is what happened. This is who changed what, when and why. And this is the exact copy of the information that I communicated to the authorities on this date.'

Archiving

Once a document is no longer active, it should be archived. This involves three things: deciding who should still have access to it (which should be decided on a need-to-know basis), ensuring that archived documents cannot be changed or deleted and giving each document a unique identity so that it can be easily retrieved if required.

There are existing archiving systems, such as Google Drive, that have built-in security features so that any alterations to a document are recorded. Some have a directed acyclic graph (DAG) function, whereby the only way to change a document is to recreate the whole thing from scratch (which is almost impossible), or source code management systems, which make documents 'undoctorable'.

Whatever archiving system you use, make sure you document why and how it is used, in case of investigation.

Internal auditing

Part of your QMS should be to establish regular, fixed dates when you check every aspect of your production and management process flows, each of which should have a log recording everything that has been done, by whom, when and why. This is your internal auditing schedule.

One such element might be your calibration log: you would need to decide how often to check that each of the devices you are using – refrigeration units, clean rooms, etc – are correctly calibrated and are working properly. You would then record what was checked and when, along with any issues that arose or were resolved.

In the event of an inspection or investigation, the reality of your business must also match the documentation you have supplied to the authorities. For example, if you have a docking area where goods come in and are checked, but which also houses a recycling unit, you must be able to justify its presence there.

Summary

- When submitting a notification, you must be able to prove that your products are fit for purpose and safe for the consumer to use.

- It is up to you to determine how to do this.

- The simplest way is to obtain ISO 9001 certification, but this has cost and time implications.

- By applying the CORE Compliance process, you can ensure that your products pass muster.

- The TPD requires you to have a set of (written) processes which ensure that your product quality is consistent and replicable.

- A legal register is a list of any regulations, standards or specifications that (might) apply to your product type in each of the countries you sell into.

- A technical file (or dossier) is a document describing that you have systems in place to ensure a consistent manufacturing process. Without one, you risk heavy penalties.

- Batch numbers must be printed on all your products for recall and surveillance purposes.

- Everything you do must be properly recorded in case of an investigation.

- Look carefully at the file structures in your information technology to ensure that there is no duplication of information.

- Another aspect of traceability is version control, which means keeping track of all iterations of, or changes to, a product or process.

- Archiving involves deciding who should still have access to a document, ensuring that it cannot be changed or deleted and giving it a unique identity so that it can be easily retrieved.

- Part of your QMS should be to establish an appropriate internal auditing schedule.

SEVEN

Risk Management

R isk management is something that is commonly avoided or completely missed. Most brands, in our experience, don't have any procedures or processes to assess the risks that they face as a business or that are inherent in their products.

Risk management is essentially a question of taking responsibility for the safety of your products. Both businesses and consumers tend to shift that responsibility onto 'the government'. Businesses think, 'The government should tell us exactly what we've got to do to make our products safe,' while consumers think, 'The government shouldn't allow a product that is unsafe to be put on the market.'

But, as we have seen, the competent authorities ('the government') don't say, 'If you do X, Y and Z, you're good,' because if you do X, Y and Z and something goes wrong, then the competent authority cannot take action against you. So, instead, they simply say, 'Your product needs to be safe and you should consider A, B and C.' It is up to you to exercise due diligence.

Worse, some brands feel that it is the consumer's responsibility to decide whether or not a product is safe for them to use. The fact is, the onus is on you, the manufacturer, to ensure that you have assessed all relevant risks – the likelihood of them happening and the impact they could have – and have built appropriate strategies to minimise the likelihood of their happening and, if they do happen, to have procedures in place to handle the consequences.

It is not only consumer safety that is at stake. If you put a product on the market that gets recalled, it can cost you a lot of money, as well as serious reputational damage. If it causes damage or harm, of course, it can also cost you millions in litigation.

The first thing to note about risk – any risk – is that it has to be seen in context, that is, in relation to some kind of goal. Essentially, a risk really is uncertainty as to the outcome of a given goal. This means, in effect, that risks can come from various directions: consumer risks, manufacturing risks, marketing risks, regulatory risks…

Note that a risk can be a positive uncertainty or a negative uncertainty. A positive uncertainty might be, for example, that you sell more of your product than you anticipated. How would you deal with that eventuality?

This chapter looks at each aspect of risk management that should be part of your due diligence process so that, if you are 'looked into' by a competent authority, you can say with confidence, 'These are all the things we do to manage our risks.'

Once again, in terms of the CORE Compliance process, it is a case of assessing your current processes (Control), identifying any gaps or potential weaknesses in them (Observe), addressing those gaps and weaknesses (React) and developing a robust risk management process going forward (Establish).

Risk assessment and risk register

Given that, like most brands, you probably already have products in the market, it is vital for you to identify the risks that you have before you can determine how to manage those risks.

Normally, when we undertake a gap analysis (see Chapter 3) and ask whether a brand has made a risk assessment or a risk register, the answer is no. In many cases, businesses don't even know what a risk register is. Most companies – certainly, the smaller ones – aren't considering risks at all. Their main concerns are whether their products taste nice and vape well. They know what chemicals are not allowed to be in them (at least, for Europe) and how to carry out an emissions test, but that tends to be the beginning and end of their consideration of risk.

A risk assessment begins with the company. Ask yourself:

- Who are your clients?

- How do you conduct business?

- Do you operate through distributors or wholesalers?

- If so, does the responsibility for notifications, for example, lie with them or with you?

- Do they have clear geographical areas into which they are entitled to sell your products?

When it comes to the products themselves, you should be asking questions such as:

- How do we create a product?

- How do we go about sourcing the ingredients?

- Who is responsible for what?

There are various ways of identifying risks, such as drawing a bow-tie or a fishbone diagram. A fairly simple method is in terms of topics. For example, 'What are our risks in terms of politics, or the economy, or the environment?'

You will also need to assess your own and your suppliers' and customers' risk 'appetite'. This means the degree of risk they are willing to accept. To take a simple example, we know that there are fatalities on the UK's roads every year, and yet most of us are willing to risk driving to get from A to B. Our 'appetite' for driving (rather than using any other form of transport or simply staying at home) is such that we are willing to accept this risk every time we get into a car. The point here is that you are never looking to make everything 100% safe, but to minimise every risk as much as is reasonably possible.

From this risk assessment you should be able to compile a risk register, which is not necessarily a list of all the potential risks your business faces, but the principal risks. (If you aren't careful, you can end up with an almost infinite number of risks, some of which are uncontrollable, such as: 'What would happen to my business if a meteor hit the Earth?')

You then need to sort those main risks using some kind of scoring mechanism based on the likelihood of something happening compared with the impact it would have. At a very simple level, for example, you might give a score of 1-3 for likelihood and 1-3 for impact. You then multiply those two scores together and those with the highest scores are your core risks.

Next, you should consider each risk in turn. Discuss them in a group, because the same risk can be described in different ways by different people. Think of the consequences of those events happening and consider a set of 'risk controls' to mitigate them. Controls include things you can do to prevent the event from happening and ways you can limit the damage they cause if they do happen.

Then, you must manage the risks, ie, actually apply the controls and make sure they are implemented. After all, there is no point in coming up with a policy unless it is actually put into practice. Some controls might at first seem 'silly' or plain annoying ('Do we really have to do that every time?'), so it is important to draw everyone's attention to both the controls and the potential consequences of the risks they are designed to mitigate, so that they are aware of and understand the reasons for them. The Royal Navy, for example, puts up big posters highlighting each of the top pilot error risks – and their likely consequences!

Compiling a risk register isn't the end of your risk management process. Once that is done, you will need to monitor and review those risks in the light of your (new) objectives: ensure that the relative 'importance' of your principal risks doesn't change, that new risks don't emerge or suddenly gain importance, or that what was once a major risk is no longer as significant.

For example, if your largest market is the UK, your principal risk will relate to the sale of products in the UK. But in six months' time, Germany might have become your biggest market, so your number one risk would drop to number two. Similarly, you may be aiming to be number one in the UK, but your objectives may change next year, which will affect the priority of risks.

Other factors that might affect your objectives – and, therefore, your risk assessment – are a change in the formulation of your product or the appearance of new knowledge, for example, regarding toxicology.

As you can see, risk assessment is a constant process as your objectives and market factors change.

Regulatory awareness

It's essential that everyone is aware of the company's risks and risk management methods and just as essential that they are aware of the regulations that might impact your products.

We discussed the regulations that apply to the vape industry in Chapters 1 and 2, and the importance of realising that it is not only the TPD that needs to be observed, but a host of other regulations as well.

It goes without saying that the markets you present your products in will also dictate the regulations you are obligated by (see Chapter 1). You might understand your products, but you might not be aware, for example, that workplace exposure limits (WELs) vary across European countries. What is right for France might be quite different from what is required in Germany and different again for the UK.

Professional advice

One way of reducing your risk – and being seen to be doing so – is to seek professional advice. If you attempt something that is not within your competence, or for which you are not qualified, such as making toxicological assessments or compiling safety data sheets (see Chapter 8), you run the risk of charges of negligence and costly litigation.

As I highlighted in the introduction, *How Safe is Your Vape?* is not intended to be a substitute for expert advice, whether that be from a toxicologist, a law firm or a regulatory specialist. It is merely a 'roadmap', showing you the way and highlighting areas that you need to consider in order to be compliant. Some aspects of this you will be able to do inhouse; for others, you will require professional help and it is a false economy not to obtain it.

This is where your legal register (see Chapter 6) and risk register (see Chapter 7) are invaluable. By identifying the regulations that are going to impact you in the market(s) you want to open and the risks that this will expose you to, you will be able to see where you need professional advice and expertise.

Single point of contact

I cannot recommend too strongly that you have one person in your organisation who is responsible for handling everything to do with regulatory compliance. This doesn't mean that they have to do everything to do with compliance themselves, but they must be the single point of contact for the competent authorities (or for specialists or professionals working on your behalf) and the only source of information that is fed back to your organisation.

This not only reduces the risks of misunderstanding, errors and duplication of information; it also streamlines your operations – which, as you know, is something that will keep the competent authorities happy.

Local representation

The competent authorities in each EU member state require you to have a local legal representative who will take responsibility for the safety of your product in that market. This might be your importer or distributor. An American brand, for example, cannot act as its own legal representative in Europe and, since Brexit, the UK no longer recognises an EU legal representative. Even Germany will not recognise a representative from another EU country.

The main idea behind this is that if something goes wrong, the EU will be able to take legal action against you via your local representative, but it also applies to product notifications. Many brands are unaware of this and suddenly have to scramble to find a local representative authorised to submit their new product notification.

The legislation also stipulates that your local distributor needs to be contracted with clear geographical guidelines, as well as financial targets. This is to prevent them from selling into other markets, and so that your products are fully traceable.

It also makes sense in terms of communication. A local representative will (presumably) speak the local language and know the local laws. Google Translate is all very well, but it is not up to the nuances of international regulations and requirements. And, if you use it and something goes wrong, you can't sue Google!

The essential point here is that you are responsible for obeying the law in the countries in which you sell your products.

There can be another plus side to employing a local representative: when EU directives, for example, are translated and 'transposed' for different member states, subtle language differences can actually create business opportunities, which your local representative might be able to take advantage of.

Product compliance files

Product compliance files are just what they say they are: a collection of documents that record the ways in which you are complying with applicable regulations. It is one thing to be compliant, and quite another to be able to demonstrate to a third party such as a competent authority that you are compliant (or have made every reasonable effort to be so).

Product compliance files should be the end result of your regulatory compliance process. Not having adequate compliance files for each of your products is a risk which has consequences if something goes wrong and the competent authorities investigate.

As we have seen, however, the vape market is becoming more educated, so that even distributors and retailers are requiring in-depth product compliance files before they will sign a contract with you.

There are varying levels of obligations within compliance files. Some documents, such as safety data sheets, are legally required to be passed down or made available to all downstream users of your products and must be accessible by emergency services (eg, in the event of a transport spill). Others, such as technical files, are simply included in case you receive an inquiry or an investigation from a competent authority.

In order to compile adequate compliance files, you need a full understanding of both your requirements and your obligations. You also need to consider the question of balancing the production of information with the need to keep information secret, the method(s) by which you will transfer them to the authorities, and the process by which you are going to update the files, while maintaining version control (see Chapter 6).

Internal auditing

You have identified your risks and built your risk register, you have made sure you are up to date in terms of regulatory awareness, you have implemented a single point of contact, and you have sought professional advice where necessary. What are you doing to ensure that this status remains valid? What are you doing to continually check that your risk assessments are appropriate and comprehensive?

It is important to realise that every single aspect of your risk management process requires constant (or periodic, at least) attention. This means that you need to build an internal auditing system that specifies how often each of those aspects is to be reviewed.

For example, you might decide to review your risk register quarterly or biannually. And for that, you might plan a half-day or full-day session. For regulatory awareness, on the other hand, you might simply make sure that you sign up to any email alerts from the competent authority, so that you are automatically notified of any changes to regulations. With regard to professional advice, you might decide to have an annual meeting with the professional(s) you are working with.

In other words, internal auditing should be treated as a business activity in its own right, requiring you to go through every aspect of your risk management strategy and attribute a procedure to each aspect. This is something that few businesses do, but it is an essential part of your compliance and due diligence processes.

In addition, your auditing procedures should be published and propagated up and down the distribution chain – to competent authorities in one direction and distributors, retailers and representatives in the other.

Summary

- Risk management is often avoided or completely missed.

- It is essentially a question of taking responsibility for the safety of your products.

- In order to determine how to manage the risks involved in their manufacture and sale, you must first identify those risks.

- This can be done by breaking them down into topics, such as politics, the economy, or the environment.

- You can never make everything 100% safe, but must minimise every risk as much as is reasonably possible.

- From your risk assessment you should compile a risk register – a list of the principal risks your business faces.

- These must then be prioritised using some kind of scoring system to arrive at your core risks.

- Consider the consequences of those events happening and consider a set of 'controls' to mitigate the risks.

- You must then manage these risks by applying the controls, making sure that everyone is aware of them, and that they are actually implemented.

- Finally, you will need to constantly monitor and review those risks in the light of changes to your objectives and to external (market) factors.

- Ensure that everyone is aware of the regulations that might impact your products (Chapter 1).

- The markets you present your products in will dictate the regulations you are obligated by.

- One way of reducing your risk – and being seen to be doing so – is to seek professional advice.

- Ensure that you have one person in your organisation who is responsible for handling everything to do with regulatory compliance – a single point of contact.

- You should compile detailed product compliance files: documents that record the ways in which you are complying with applicable regulations.

- Every single aspect of your risk management process requires constant (or periodic, at least) attention.

- This internal auditing process should be treated as a business activity in its own right.

EIGHT

Classification, Labelling And Packaging

As with many other aspects of vape product manufacture and marketing, many small businesses started out simply copying the labelling and packaging of the market leaders on an, 'If it's good enough for them, it's good enough for me,' basis. In most other areas, manufacturers have upped their game and made sure they are complying with the current regulations, but there is still a lack of understanding in the industry generally of the requirements regarding classification, labelling and packaging (CLP). This applies particularly to the classification of hazards and how that determines what information must be shown on packaging or labelling or included in product information.

This aspect of regulatory compliance is driven in part by the TPD, but in the main by Regulation (EC) 1272/2008 of the European Parliament and of the Council of 16 December 2008 on the classification, labelling and packaging of substances and mixtures – known as the CLP regulation – which aligns the EU system of classification, labelling and packaging with the Globally Harmonised System of Classification and Labelling of Chemicals (GHS) agreed at United Nations level.

In this chapter, I will explain how to go about classifying your products in order to determine the information that needs to be on the packaging or labelling – in terms of pictograms and symbols, for example – or in a product leaflet or other document.

As before, your overall approach to CLP should follow the CORE Compliance process: Control your current processes, Observe any gaps or potential weaknesses in them, React to those gaps and weaknesses, and Establish robust systems that will ensure your continuous compliance.

Classification

The labelling and packaging of a product is driven by the classification of the hazardous chemicals in the e-liquid, and the quantities of those chemicals that it contains. It may be that a tiny amount of a certain chemical is not considered hazardous to human health, but once it exceeds a specified threshold, it is.

Throughout the EU, these thresholds are published by the ECHA in the form of Excel tables, which are updated regularly. From these tables, by taking into account the amount of each substance within your formulation and referencing the harmonised classifications for each substance, you can determine your product classification, as required by the 2006 REACH Regulation (EC 1907/2006). This is known as your 'harmonised classification and labelling' (CLH), which must be made available to all downstream users.

The classification is essentially a measure of the toxicity of your product, which may be dermal (through skin contact), oral (by ingestion) or – particularly in the case of vape products – by inhalation.

Toxicity is measured on a four-point scale: products that are 'highly toxic and severely irritating' are classed as Category 1 products; 'moderately toxic and moderately irritating' products are Category 2; 'slightly toxic and slightly irritating' products are Category 3; and products that are 'practically non-toxic and not an irritant' are Category 4.[4]

Depending on the product, there may be other types of hazards, such as inflammability or allergens that can cause reactions in the user.

---

4   https://echa.europa.eu

Your final product classification will determine what statements, warnings, pictograms, etc, must appear on your labelling, packaging and in other product information.

As you might imagine, working out your product classification is no simple task – and one that may require specialist help (see Chapter 7).

Pictograms and symbols

There are eight CLP pictograms that are applicable to consumer products:

 Acute toxicity (severe)

 Harmful skin irritation, serious eye irritation, acute toxicity (harmful)

 Flammable gases, flammable liquids, flammable solids, flammable aerosols, organic peroxides, self-reactive, pyrophoric, self-heating, contact with water emits flammable gas

 Explosive, self-reactive, organic peroxide

Harmful to the environment, hazard to the aquatic environment

 Oxidising gases, oxidising liquids, oxidising solids

 Respiratory sensitiser, mutagen, carcinogen, reproductive toxicity, systemic target organ toxicity, aspiration hazard

 Corrosive (causes severe skin burns and eye damage), serious eye damage

Your product classification will also generate a 'signal word' – which is either 'warning' or 'danger', depending on the hazard level – as well as one or more 'hazard statements', 'precautionary statements' and 'supplemental statements'. Examples of hazard statements are:

- Causes serious eye damage.

- Toxic if swallowed.

- May cause allergy or asthma symptoms or breathing difficulties if inhaled.

A precautionary statement applicable to a vape product might be, 'If swallowed, call a doctor immediately,' and a typical supplemental statement is, 'To avoid risks to human health and the environment, comply with the instructions for use.'

In the UK, the precautionary statements are driven by the TPD rather than the CLP. So, for example, your products will need to carry the warning: 'This product contains nicotine. Nicotine is a highly addictive substance.'

If your product or packaging is too small to carry multiple pictograms and/or statements, you can normally choose the statement or pictogram that is most relevant to your product and articulates the highest level of warning. For example, you are unlikely to show the statement, 'If inhaled, move the victim to fresh air'! The full set of pictograms and statements must be included on your safety data sheet (see below).

Some warnings or statements apply to use in a workplace, which will not be relevant in terms of consumer use, but might be relevant to your wholesalers, distributors and retailers who will be handling large quantities of your products (see 'Regional requirements' below).

Other symbols that might need to appear on the labelling or packaging are the CE (or UKCA) mark (see Chapter 1) and the WEEE (waste electrical and electronic equipment recycling) symbol. The latter would not be required on a liquid product, but would on any disposable device, and even on a tank if filled and sold separately.

Unique formula identifier

A unique formula identifier (UFI), a sixteen-digit code, was introduced in 2020 and will become mandatory on the label of all products classified as containing health or physical hazards from 2025. Importers and downstream users placing such products on the market must provide the UFI, along with other product-specific information, to poison centres.

Regional requirements

As we mentioned before in connection with local representation (see Chapter 7), if you are selling into non-English-speaking countries, you will obviously need to have information in the local language(s).

You will also need to consider the handling and storage of your products by transport companies, wholesalers, distributors and retailers, which means being aware of WELs. These can vary from country to country, even within the EU. France and Germany, for example, have much lower WELs for certain chemicals than most other EU member states. France also requires recyclable products to carry the 'Triman' logo.

Other countries may require recycling-related pictograms or symbols, especially for products containing batteries. Your local representative should be able to advise you on this, but also make your own investigations to ensure that you stay on the right side of the law.

Imagery and artwork

In terms of imagery and artwork, you need to go through a fairly robust due diligence process to ensure that products don't reach the market with non-compliant packaging. We have recently seen an increase in the number of product seizures being carried out by competent authorities or trading standards organisations for contravention of the regulations in this regard.

Because vape products are age-restricted, both the TPD and the CLP stipulate that the imagery and artwork you use on the packaging of your products must not be 'child-appealing'. Anything that could be deemed to be attractive to minors, such as a 'cartoony' design, is out of scope.

There are also restrictions on the way in which you can depict food. So, if you have an e-liquid with, say, an apple pie flavour, you will need to be very careful how you present that in your artwork. Above all, your design mustn't mislead the consumer into thinking that your e-liquid or e-cigarette is a food or cosmetic product.

There is no requirement to put the kind of images that are compulsory on cigarette packets on vape products... yet. There have, however, been calls for imposing plain packaging so, as ever, it is up to you to constantly monitor the regulatory landscape to make sure that you don't fall foul of any new or revised legislation.

There are templates available for the design of your packaging and labelling, which will ensure that you include all the necessary elements. Even if you don't use exactly the same format, these will at least make it clear what needs to be there.

Documentation

As well as designing the packaging and labelling of your products, you will need to consider the documentation that must accompany them. Most important of all is the safety data sheet.

Safety data sheet

Formerly the material safety data sheet (MSDS), the safety data sheet (SDS) is the key document you need to produce. In most cases, this is the first document that any competent authority or customs office will want to see when your product is coming into their territory. It is, therefore, absolutely crucial that this document is complete and that all the required information is presented in the correct format.

Each and every SDS must be renewed, or at least reviewed, every two years. Even if the formulation of a product doesn't change, you must still produce an updated version (eg, Version 1.1) to demonstrate that the SDS is up to date. Note that an SDS is specific to the formulation and not just to the product, so if a product exists in different nicotine levels, for example, you must have a separate SDS for each formulation.

An SDS has sixteen sections and Section 2 relates to hazardous identification, classification of the substance or mixture, and label elements. This specifies 99% of the information that needs to go on the product label in accordance with CLP requirements.

Leaflets

Whereas the CLP allows certain products whose contents do not exceed 125ml to be sold without a leaflet, the TPD requires a leaflet to be included with all vape products, without exception – even tanks sold separately with no liquid in them. The leaflet needs to include information on the toxicity and addictiveness of the product, any adverse effects that might be experienced, warnings for specific risk groups (see 'Specific groups' below), instructions on keeping the product out of the reach of children, any contra-indications (see below), and contact information for the manufacturer, among other things.

For the UK market, if the product packaging can include all the above sufficiently, there is, in theory, no need to include a leaflet. However, because the TPD specifies a requirement for a leaflet, trading standards will expect to see a leaflet and you may have to justify its omission if questioned. It is, therefore, advisable to include one.

If your product is required to display a CE or UKCA or WEEE mark, those symbols must also be present on any documentation provided with the product, including the leaflet.

Should you decide to produce a generic leaflet for multiple products rather than individual leaflets for each item in order to save costs, make sure that it includes all the required information for all the products to which it applies.

Child-resistant

Not surprisingly, there is a requirement for your product packaging to be child-resistant. As with so many

HOW SAFE IS YOUR VAPE?

other regulations, however, there are no specifics as to how you might achieve this; it is up to you to take reasonable steps to ensure that children cannot readily access your products.

Whereas the bottles containing e-liquid must conform to ISO 8317, devices are not subject to specific testing regimes. In fact, although on a cursory reading of the TPD you could be forgiven for assuming that both refill container and device need to be childproof, it is currently only refill containers that are subject to that requirement.

Requirements do vary across markets, however, with the Scandinavian countries being particularly stringent in their demands. To market a disposable, or even refillable, device in Denmark, for instance, you must produce 'proof' that it is child-resistant. If the authorities are not satisfied by that, the product will simply be taken off the market.

Tamper-evident packaging

According to the TPD, the packaging of vape products must also be 'tamper-evident'. In other words, it must be obvious if anyone has, say, opened a bottle of e-liquid. However, products that don't contain any liquid (ie, devices) do not need tamper-evident packaging, because there is nothing that can be tampered with.

In the case of bottles, the solution is fairly simple: a cap with a breakable ring, for example, or you could package the product in a vacuum-sealed sleeve or pouch.

Specific groups and contraindications

As mentioned above, your packaging or information leaflet must contain information relating to use by specific groups, such as pregnant and breastfeeding women and people with diabetes, heart problems or asthma, as well as a clear instruction to keep the product out of the reach of children.

Depending on the ingredients of your e-liquid, there might also be allergy implications, so you would need to include a warning such as: 'Contains substance X. May produce an allergic reaction.'

Your packaging and/or leaflet must also include contraindications, advising consumers against using the product if they have particular ailments or suffer from, say, nausea.

Note that, whereas tobacco products are not required to include such information, vape products are.

Health claims

The TPD contains clear instructions on what can be claimed for vape products and what cannot be claimed. The main point here is that you cannot claim they are cessation products. They are not intended to help people give up smoking. Nor can you claim that they are safer than tobacco products.

If you choose to market them as medicinal products that are prescribed by doctors as a cessation tool or nicotine replacement therapy, you will have to take extra precautions regarding any health claims – as well as undertake more extensive testing, which can be costly.

Even the product name cannot make the consumer think that it is less harmful than tobacco products or, indeed, than any other vape product, so terms such as 'light', 'low tar' and 'low nicotine' are unacceptable. Your products cannot be described as 'energising', 'vitalising', 'rejuvenating' or anything similar. Nor can you claim that they have any kind of environmental advantage over other products, eg, 'Less harmful to the environment than X.'

Finally, you aren't allowed to include any promotions such as 'Buy one, get one free' or a code that entitles you to money off your next purchase.

Article 13 of the TPD provides a complete list of what is not allowed in terms of product description and presentation.

Summary

- The labelling and packaging of a product is driven by the classification of the hazardous chemicals in the e-liquid, and the amounts that it contains.

- The classification is essentially a measure of the toxicity of your product.

- Your final product classification will determine what statements, warnings, pictograms, etc, must appear on your labelling, packaging and in other product information.

- Your product classification will also generate a 'signal word', which is either 'warning' or 'danger', depending on the hazard level.

- Other symbols that might need to appear on the labelling or packaging are the CE (or UKCA) mark and the WEEE mark.

- If you are selling into non-English-speaking countries, all information will need to be in the local language.

- Be aware of WELs, which can vary from country to country, even within the EU.

- The imagery and artwork you use on the packaging of your products must not be 'child-appealing'.

- The most important document to accompany your products is the SDS.

- Every SDS must be renewed, or at least reviewed, every two years.

- The TPD requires a leaflet to be included with all vape products.

- There is a requirement for your product packaging to be child-resistant.

- According to the TPD, the packaging of vape products must be 'tamper-evident'.

- Your packaging or information leaflet must also contain information relating to use by specific groups and relevant contraindications.

- The TPD stipulates that no health claims can be made for vape products.

NINE

Consumer Safety And Post-Market Surveillance

Regulatory compliance doesn't end once your products are sold. You are also required to have 'adequately robust' processes in place to handle any adverse events that might be caused by their use, to recall products if necessary, and to provide the competent authorities with consumer and market data relating to your products.

As before, make sure that your safety and surveillance strategy incorporates the CORE Compliance process.

Adverse effects tracking

As we have seen (under Observe in Chapter 3), the TPD states that, in order to ensure appropriate

HOW SAFE IS YOUR VAPE?

market surveillance by member states, manufacturers, importers and distributors must operate an appropriate system for monitoring and recording suspected adverse effects and inform the competent authorities about any such effects so that appropriate remedial action can be taken. I have outlined what the term 'appropriate' means in practice.

In reality, the market surveillance undertaken by some EU member states is less than rigorous. Certain countries, however, including Germany and Ireland, as well as the UK, are proactive in this respect.

The essential thing is, therefore, that you determine what system is appropriate for the size of your business in each country or region. This is something a lot of companies cut corners on, but if something goes wrong and you don't have an adequate tracking process, you can be in big trouble.

Severity rating

The TPD also requires you to record the severity of any reaction or other adverse event (AE). These are commonly graded on a scale of 1 to 5, as follows:

- Grade 1 – mild AE

- Grade 2 – moderate AE

- Grade 3 – severe AE

- Grade 4 – life-threatening or disabling AE

- Grade 5 – death related to AE

Software solutions

This means that, in place of a telephone number and an Excel spreadsheet, you might need a software program that will steer those complaints into a report that will allow you to adequately assess them.

Such a program would need to take into account not only language differences, but also variations in the way adverse events might be reported. To take a simple example: one person might say that they have experienced a 'tickly throat', another a 'scratchy throat', a third an 'itchy throat', and a fourth a 'sore throat'; but in terms of your adverse events reporting, these should all be reported in the same category. And the same might apply to each of the other twenty-three languages of the European Union.

Essentially, your system needs to be able to identify whether the problem is due to a batch failure, an incorrect formulation, a storage issue, or some other failing in the production, distribution or retail process; and whether a product recall is necessary (see below).

GDPR

Because your tracking system will be dealing with personally identifiable (health) information, this will have an impact on your General Data Protection Regulation (GDPR) registration. You may need a higher level of security and more sophisticated processes to ensure that those data aren't leaked.

In our experience, a lot of companies are not even doing enough even at the base level of GDPR, let alone making their systems robust enough to handle confidential health data.

Product recall protocols

If your adverse events tracking system is not adequate or robust, your products could be recalled by a competent authority before you are even able to identify the problem, let alone take any remedial action, such as recalling a particular batch. To add insult to injury, the authority will likely charge you for the privilege of having them recall your products for you!

Europe, for example, has a system called RAPEX (Rapid Exchange of Information), which is connected to all the enforcement bodies throughout the EU, and in certain non-member countries too. RAPEX can be triggered by all kinds of non-compliance issues, such as failure to include a leaflet, but it is most likely to be triggered when a series of adverse events in connection with a particular product are reported.

There is no European standard for the circumstances under which RAPEX is triggered or the amount of time you are allowed before it is invoked; it depends which country you are dealing with (the Health Service Executive [HSE] in Ireland are renowned for triggering RAPEX at the slightest provocation), and even, in some cases, the individual enforcement officer or agent you are dealing with – they might be inclined to be more or less lenient or might simply have had a good or bad day!

The important thing is that your tracking system should be ahead of the game, so that not only do you avoid the cost and loss of sales that result from an imposed recall, but also the associated reputational damage – because the vape industry is such that pretty soon *everyone* will know that your products have been 'RAPEXed'. In fact, because every single enforcement body throughout Europe is automatically notified of any initiation of RAPEX, you could find that your products are pulled by every country in Europe.

You may be advised that this is taking place, or you may not. If you are contacted by a competent authority in relation to complaints or AE reports, you should be in a position to put your hand up and say, 'OK, that's our mistake and we will initiate an immediate product recall. We know how many thousands of units were in that market, we have a single distributor, we can control the product withdrawal and it will be done within X weeks.' In most cases, that will be enough to appease them.

This requires you to have robust product recall protocols – established procedures that you can snap into action at a moment's notice.

Even if you do have efficient and effective recall protocols, the cost of a product recall can run into the tens or even hundreds of thousands of pounds/euros. Which means that you should be looking at taking out product recall insurance.

Annual sales data

Another robust system you need to have in place is one for recording your annual sales data, broken down not only into the different markets you are selling into, but also into every stock keeping unit (SKU) of every product you sell (eg, not just 'strawberry' or 'banana' flavours, but 'strawberry 3mg', 'strawberry 6mg', and so on). Therefore, if you have ten flavours and each one comes in three nicotine strengths, you will need to produce annual sales data for thirty SKUs. If you are selling into ten countries, you will need 300 separate sets of sales data. If you have hundreds of SKUs and are selling in every EU member state...

As you can see, compiling annual sales data can be quite a complex task, so you should make sure that you manage it regularly rather than leaving it until a couple of weeks from the deadline and having to scramble frantically to pull all the required data together.

For this, you might need an enterprise resource planning (ERP) system rather than a basic spreadsheet that requires manual inputting and calculation.

European data filings should usually be made through the EU-CEG and should be based on your initial product notification. Deadlines vary from country to country, but are generally between January and May (this is another thing to have embedded in your system). In most cases, you have three months' 'grace' in which to submit your data. In some, there is no leeway at all. The Polish authorities, for example, will fine you (and/or remove your products from the market) if you fail to submit your annual sales data on time; and it is likely that other EU member states will follow suit.

Consumer studies

There is generally no requirement to conduct consumer studies for your products, although Poland recently made it mandatory to do so. If you do so, you are obliged to submit the results along with your annual sales data.

The idea behind this is that you engage with your consumers to find out what flavours they prefer (see below), what their age group and gender is, etc. This not only helps you to sell more products, but also helps the authorities to monitor usage and check that, for example, there is no underage use. It is, therefore, likely that the requirement for consumer studies will scale up as the regulations mature. In any case, as a responsible manufacturer, you should be commissioning consumer studies – at least into consumer preferences and youth uptake (see below).

As in other areas of compliance, there are templates that will help you conduct such studies. These can be downloaded either free or for a small charge.

Youth uptake

An important study to conduct (and one that will earn you 'Brownie points') is the extent of youth uptake of your products, since the authorities are particularly keen to know whether vaping is being adopted by people under the legal age for tobacco use. Again, this is an area that is likely to be legislated in the (near) future.

Flavour preferences

Both you (who are concerned with increasing sales) and the authorities (who are concerned with safeguarding consumer health) will want to know which flavours are 'trending' among which consumer groups. You will also need to know which countries have banned flavours (other than tobacco and menthol).

Market relevance

It should go without saying that you will only conduct consumer studies that are relevant to the markets
you are selling into. (You wouldn't submit a consumer
study conducted in France to the authorities in Poland
or anywhere else.) Beyond that, you should ensure
that the sample you use is consistent with the relevant
market, ie, with the population you are targeting your
products at. A problem we have come across in America, for example, is that many of the studies submitted
with PMTAs are global rather than focused on the
American market.

Summary

- You are required to have 'adequately robust'
  processes in place to monitor and record any
  AEs that your products might cause, to recall
  them if necessary, and to provide the competent
  authorities with consumer and market data
  relating to your products.

- The TPD requires you to record the severity of
  any reaction or other AE.

- For this you might require a specialised
  software program.

- Because your tracking system will be dealing with confidential information, this will have an impact on your GDPR registration.

- You should have robust product recall protocols that can be put into action at a moment's notice.

- Another robust system you need to have in place is one for recording your annual sales data.

- As a responsible manufacturer, you should be commissioning consumer studies into consumer preferences and youth uptake at the least.

- Consumer studies must be relevant to the markets you are selling into, and the sample you use should be consistent with the population you are targeting your products at.

Conclusion

As I hope this book has shown, it is now essential for any vape brand owner to take regulatory compliance as seriously as marketing and to attribute an appropriate budget and resources to it. Gone are the days when compliance meant simply copying what the leading brands were doing and hoping for the best.

The regulations are only going to get more complicated as the enforcement bodies become more educated and consumers become more demanding and discerning. The bar is rising year on year. But you can raise your game and stay on top of the requirements by applying the CORE Compliance methodology outlined in this book:

- Control

- Observe

- React

- Establish

CORE Compliance applies to six key areas of regulatory compliance, which are present in all regulatory frameworks in the UK, Europe and North America: product data; analytical data; risk management; quality management; classification, labelling and packaging; and consumer safety and post-market surveillance.

In each area, it is a matter of first establishing your current compliant status (or not, as the case may be), then reviewing the data, building a compliance strategy based on those data, and, finally, implementing the strategy.

As I have mentioned, this book is written in layman's terms to help non-technical, non-scientific brand owners better understand their baseline obligations. It provides you with a basic roadmap of what you need to do to become and remain fully compliant. It is not a bible. It is not a replacement for reading and understanding the regulations. It is not an exhaustive and foolproof method, and it is not a substitute for hiring specialist consultancies or legal representation, which are essential if you are to safeguard your business and build your brand.

Remember, though, that it is not up to the government to safeguard consumers; it is up to you. It is your responsibility to do everything you can to reduce risk – both to the consumer and to your business.

Resources

Among the resources provided by Arcus Compliance are:

CORE Compliance Health Check – a scorecard system that allows you to get an idea of where you currently sit from a product stewardship and compliance perspective. It's entirely free and can be completed on: https://arcuscompliance.com/health-check

VAPETOX – an online screening tool that will screen for banned substances and provide you with an aggregated CAS presentation for your products.

VAPEVIGIL – a unique, vape-industry-specific software program for recording any safety concerns related to your products, identifying the cause, and enabling you to respond rapidly and effectively.

Acknowledgements

I'd like to thank everyone that had an input into the book, particularly John Walker, John Donoghue, Keelie Turnbull, Hannah Fury, Aaron Farmer, Sebastian Wisniewski, Robert Sidebottom and the rest of the Arcus Compliance team. Thanks also go to John Dunne and the UKVIA for their help over the past few years.

I'd also like to thank all the haters who have, over the years, fuelled me to achieve greater things. You know who you are!

The Author

Lee Bryan is one of the best-known names in the vaping industry, having gained a reputation for truly caring for his clients and delivering on his promises since he founded Arcus Compliance with John Walker in 2017. Over the past decade, Lee has worked with some of the largest and best-known vaping brands in the world, as well as collaborating closely with decision-makers, regulatory bodies and enforcement agencies.

Motivated by the experience of losing his father, grandfather and grandmother to smoking-related illnesses, Lee decided to write a book for the industry's pioneers – those who had also experienced the damage that combustible tobacco can do, those who were passionately trying to give consumers an alternative to combustibles and who needed advice on how to remain in the game.

The thought of writing a book never occurred to Lee until 2018 when he began working with Daniel Priestley, who inspired and motivated him to put finger to keypad. The result is a book whose focus is on ensuring that consumer protection is at the forefront of everything the industry does, that its entrepreneurial spirit is still evident in five years' time, to keep the industry 'boutique' and provide the best, safest and widest portfolio of vapour products possible without handing control back to Big Tobacco.

⊕ www.arcuscompliance.com

in www.linkedin.com/in/leejohnbryan